Drumming Up Vibrations

GW00725072

By
Paul Francis

An autobiography of a musician's career starting in the 60's

ISBN   978-0-9569722-0-0

Printed by The Lavenham Press Ltd, Arbons House,
47 Water Street, Lavenham, Suffolk, CO10 9RN

First published in Great Britain by Twizz Publications,
Orchard Bungalow, London Road,
Great Horkesley, Colchester, Essex CO6 4DA

Above: Paul Francis and Tony Jackson

This book is dedicated to Tony Jackson,
a great vocalist, bass player and friend, who gave me the opportunity
to experience the 60's music scene.

Contents

ACCESS ALL AREAS

NAME
PAUL FRANCIS
Artist

JAHRE
CHIPE

CITY in the CITY
1991
POPERINGE   MAEKEBLIJDEZAAL
NAAM: PAUL FRANCIS

ARTIEST

ARTIST
'94
ROCK FESTIVAL
STEVE HARLEY   kl. 11.00-16.00

BACK
STAGE

OPEN AIR
ESBJERG GLAM ROCK
FESTIVAL

Foreword

Paul Francis has been a professional drummer for over fifty years, working with a wide range of artists including:

Rolf Harris, Bill Wyman, Jack Bruce, Jet Harris, Gilbert O'Sullivan, Maggie Bell, Steve Harley and Cockney Rebel, Suzi Quatro, Mick Ronson, Chris Spedding, John Paul Jones, Albert Lee, Tony Jackson and The Vibrations, Billie Davis, Dickie Pride, Carl Wayne, Marion Montgomery, Screaming Lord Sutch, Wee Willie Harris, Fuzzy Duck, Tranquility, Jimmy Justice, Craig Douglas, John Walker, Tucky Buzzard, Geno Washington, Joe Pasquale.

Since 1982 Paul has been running his own drum school, Orchard Percussion Studio, near Colchester, Essex. Paul has written several drum tuition books and DVDs as well as a number of graded drum kit examination pieces for the Trinity Guildhall School of Music. Paul also released his own CD Pablo.

Acknowledgements

A special friend, Rose Halls, kept suggesting and encouraging me to put my experiences down on paper.   Thank you Rosie.

Special thanks to my mother and father who always supported me and never insisted that I should get 'a proper job'!   My father gave me so much encouragement and best of all his time; he was always there for me.

I also thank my tutors, the many musicians, artists and associated people I have met along my way as a drummer for giving me the lifetime experience that I dreamt of.

Big thanks to my cousin Stuart for also suggesting I put pen to paper, my brother Geoff and all those friends who have helped in getting the book together including Ron Long, Denis Thompson, Marianna Buisel, Tony Lukyn, Trevor Duplock, Bernie Hagley, John Ledbetter, Pat Crisp, Dave Brown, Keith Gladman, Terry Shaddick, Kevin McCarthy, Chris Teeder.

Many grateful thanks to Lavenham Press in particular Lisa Hibbert for her designs and Bill Byford for helping to put this book together.

A very special thank you to Goldie for her time and dedicated assistance, without which this book would not have come to fruition.

Chapter 1

Early Years

Two gentlemen arrived from the Funeral Directors; slowly they manoeuvred the body bag containing the body of Tony Jackson down the small narrow stairs and into the street below. A sudden realisation hit me that my friend Tony was no longer with us and that millions of fans around the world would be deeply saddened on hearing the news of his death. From 1964 until 1967 we had enjoyed many good times recording and touring around England and Europe.

As a child, death is hard to accept; as the years go by you realise the body is only flesh and one's soul lives on. As a young child my first encounter with death was a pet rabbit which I had found abandoned on some waste ground. Its fur was very matted so I took it home to clean it up. I called him Binky. We would play hide and seek in the garden and when he died I was very upset.

We lived in a terraced house, number 8, Ash Tree Close, Shirley, Croydon, Surrey. It was a small cul-de-sac with an unmade road from where it had been bombed during the war. I was born on 11th October 1947 in Stone Park Nursing Home, Beckenham, Kent. By all accounts I was a bit of a grizzler as a child. I think some of that would have been due to my getting car sickness. I had a very happy childhood. My brother Geoff and I would play but as he was seven years older he was soon off out with his mates so I found my own circle of friends. My first school was called Monks Orchard about half a mile by road but the quicker option was through an alleyway at the top of our cul-de-sac.

I remember my first day at school very well. My mother took me. As we entered the school via the back gate we passed classrooms leading on to the playground. Before I knew what was going on the lady teacher grabbed my hand and said to my mother "don't worry, he will be okay" and walked me away. I remember being very upset and not wanting to go with this lady who I did not know. Looking back now it was probably the start of my insecurities of being with people who I don't know. I did however settle in okay and I can remember stepping in to help someone being bullied in the playground. There were two or three boys onto one so a friend and I evened up the numbers. We saw the bullies off and made a lot of new friends in the process.

People often ask me when I started playing the drums. I think it was about the age of 5 or 6. I can remember two teachers standing in the doorway of our classroom.

One of the teachers produced a drum and played a rhythm. The drum was then passed around the classroom and the teacher asked if any one of us could repeat the rhythm that had been played. As I listened to my classmates all trying one by one I thought "I can do that". As the drum worked its way to me I tried tapping the rhythm out on my legs. When it was my turn I was able to play the rhythm. A girl also managed to play it. The teacher said that we would have a drum each and play in front of the stage during the school play. And that was my first introduction to the drum. I suppose that would have been my first public gig with an audience made up of parents.

The alleyway from our house had long gardens backing onto it which were an endless source of fun. My friend Clive's garden was very overgrown at the bottom end which made it even more fun for playing in. We used to buy fireworks, bangers mostly, around Guy Fawkes Night. We would place a banger in a jar and fill it with soot. We would always buy the largest one we could afford. The firework was lit often with an extended fuse made out of paper to give us time to leg it before it exploded. When it went off it sounded really loud. Then we would run back to see what was left of the jar with soot everywhere.

Another trick was to tie a banger to a dart, light it and then throw it at someone's front door. The banger would go off and we would be running up the road with the owner shouting after us. Later we would go back and often the dart was still in the door, so we could retrieve it and use it for a new destination. Another favourite firework was a rocket which produced a lit up parachute when it descended with a plastic soldier attached to it.

To my mother's disgust, I would often find dead birds which I would bring home to bury them in the garden. I did not like to see these birds lying there and thought they deserved to be buried. My mother was horrified to find out from my nan that I had a mouse's head in a matchbox in my bedroom. I once found a stuffed monkey on a stick at a nearby building site. I thought it looked great fun. My mother and her friend were talking in the front room so I held this monkey up at the window and to my delight frightened the life out of them. My mother made me take it back straight away.

I can remember finding a slow worm. I did keep some pet mice in the shed but they bred too fast so it was rabbits after that in the garden with a hutch and run. I also found a half bald chicken with a bulging chest which I named Fred. One day it laid an egg which I proudly gave to mum insisting she ate it for breakfast. The state of poor Fred was enough to put anyone off eggs for life. Poor mum passed on that one saying she would eat it later.

I recollect that I seemed to be a little accident prone as a child. On one occasion my mum had gone to visit her sister for the weekend and dad and I planned on going into Elmers End that day. Dad said we would go on his bike. I sat on the back while he pedalled. "Don't forget to keep your feet away from the wheels, son" dad said. Famous last words. The ride was about a mile or so and we were just outside the Odeon cinema when my foot went straight through the spokes of the back wheel. We came to an abrupt halt all over the road right in front of the cinema. The cinema doorman, who was wearing a big red uniform, came rushing over to help and said we had better go in the cinema foyer. After freeing my foot from the wheel we went inside and sat on the couch. We pulled back my sock and were horrified to see that all the skin had been taken off my foot. That was my first encounter in the hospital. My mother arrived home to find me with a bandaged foot with the words "I've only been away for two days NOW what have you done?"

My next hospital visit was to remove a large splinter which had gone down the back of my fingernail. This had happened as I bent down to pick up the dog and my fingers scraped down the sideboard. The nurse asked if I wanted some pain killers which I refused, and then cut my nail right down each side of the splinter. The pain was excruciating, but I kept quiet. She told my father I had been very brave, and he bought me some sweets on the way home as a treat.

My next hospital visit, I was getting used to this by now, was while making up the bonfire in Clive's garden ready for Guy Fawkes Night. I picked up a piece of wood which I went to throw hard against an old door on the bonfire not noticing a nail which went right through my finger. There I was sitting in a hospital waiting room with this grotty old piece of wood and a rusty nail through my finger. I remember feeling very embarrassed sitting there holding this lump of wood.

My nan and granddad had owned a holiday chalet in Swalecliffe near Herne Bay which passed down to my father. All four of us would travel down in our 1937 Austin Ruby car with the suitcase strapped on to the spare wheel at the back. I loved that car; it had belonged to my grandfather. It had little yellow indicators that would appear from the side of the vehicle to indicate left or right. I can still remember the number plate AVB 395 which is more than I can say about my present car.

The car was never fast, in fact while going round a roundabout once I fell out and managed to catch up and jump back in. I had opened the door previously to talk to friends while dad was in the shop and not really closed it. In the end mum refused to go out in it. The final straw was being overtaken by a push bike on a hill. "I'm not going in that car any more" she said and made dad buy a new car.

For the journey to the chalet Geoff and I would be given comics to read in the back, but no sooner had we set off than we would be playing around. Dad would wave his hands at us to stop and read the comics. Geoff went into the Royal Navy at Ganges when he was 15 so then there was just the three of us.

Often arriving at night when it was dark the gas lamps would be lit. These gave off a very distinctive smell and a very homely

Above: Chalet
August 1955

and warm feeling as you went in. The settee pulled out and made a double bed for my parents and I slept in a blanket box with the lid propped up. We were very lucky as the chalet was in the middle of the front row with acres of playing field in front with the sea just a few hundred yards away to the left. A small putting green was added several years later. We had an outside washstand with a bowl and a food safe. Water was collected by large enamel jugs from an outside tap. There was a toilet block with showers and a site shop. To the rear of the chalets there was a caravan site, where my Aunt Vera and Uncle Harold and my cousins Miriam and Susan had a caravan. Susan who was my age was very good fun and more often than not we would finish up in the amusement arcade on the site trying to win a toy from the crane machine.

I must admit to being hooked on slot machines and I was always trying to work out just how far to bring my thumb back to flick the ball round and hopefully get a win which was never very often. If the machine was paying out too much the man in the corner office who gave change would come out with a screwdriver and adjust it. Occasionally one machine would stick on win and the pennies would keep paying out. We would look over to see if the man had noticed what was going on but he never missed very much.

The gents' toilets on the campsite had pay cubicles and one had a loose box on the door so you could retrieve the pennies from it. Another source of income was to collect milk bottles and take them back to the shop and get the return money back on them.

More often than not when we arrived I would jump from the car and head straight to the amusement arcade. By the time mum and dad had walked 100 yards to the chalet

14

from the car park I had lost my money on the machines. I once told mum I had lost my pocket money. Never mind dear she replied we will go and look for it for you thinking I'd lost it in the playing field. I even made a cardboard slot machine at home and tried to get everyone to have a go.

In the evening bingo was played in the amusement arcade and I must stress we are not talking about a large building here but as a child everything seems huge. I was too young to play bingo but would watch all the grown-ups. As the winner shouted "house" the bingo man who had a wart on his nose would check the card and shout "there he do sit, the winner". Then teddy bears or some other prize would be handed down from a centre stand. My brother was quite lucky winning several times.

We very often had fish and chips for tea and once while eating some cod a bone became stuck in my throat. It would not shift so I was taken to the local hospital to have it removed with a long pair of tweezers.

I have always been interested in wildlife and loved looking for nests, just to see how many I could find. There were many house sparrows around then, and they would nest in the farm buildings adjacent to the camp site. Song thrush eggs were so blue and bright. I love to hear the song thrush and the blackbird sing.

In later years my father bought a small rowing boat. My friend Paul Norman, dad and I went out one day. Dad was still wearing his T shirt and watch. He instructed us to move over a bit to even up the weight. Well, as we both moved poor dad was catapulted out of the boat, glasses and all.

Back at Ash Tree Close, one day Clive and I were playing Hide and Seek in the alleyway. Clive had a homemade bow and arrow and was hiding in the bushes and as I crept along the alley, bang, this arrow hit me right in the eye. I remember being angry and telling Clive what a fool he was. But who would have thought it would hit me in the eye. We played a bit more then I went home. Dad took one look at me and said "What's wrong with your eye? Let me have a look." On inspection he could see it was bleeding, so it was off to the hospital. Here we go again, I thought. When I looked in the mirror, the arrow had hit the white of my eye and peeled it off in one place.

The outcome was I finished up going to Moorfields Eye Hospital in London for several months for treatment. They told me that if the arrow had been a fraction over I would have lost the sight in that eye. Boy, was I lucky.

Once when I was cycling to school I was knocked off my bike by a car. The back wheel was buckled. I think the man who brought me home was more shaken up than I was having driven into me. He came straight out from a side street.

On Saturdays I would go to Saturday Morning Pictures for the Westerns, which were always good fun.

My next school was Marian Vian which was about a mile and a half from home. I used to bike there or walk. I remember enjoying art classes. It was during my time there that I developed the habit of tapping. Usually a lot on the table at dinner time using the knives as sticks. Mum would tell me to stop that tapping. In the end she told my father to get me a drum as the tapping was driving her mad.

Dad bought me a snare drum made of red plastic with a small cymbal attached. It was an Eric Delaney model with black tripod legs. I loved it. I had tried a plastic trumpet the year before, but I did not fancy that. A drum was really very appealing. I had pictures of Buddy Rich, Louie Bellson and Gene Krupa around my bedroom walls. They all had huge drum kits which looked amazing compared to my one drum! It was only years later that I discovered what great players they were.

My brother gave me an acoustic guitar one Christmas. But the drum always took preference. If we went to watch a carnival I would love the sound of the drums in the Sea Cadets. As they turned the corner towards where we were standing they sounded so exciting. The big bass drum and the snare drums were an amazing sound.

About four roads from our house was a large green. One day while looking for something to do I noticed that the last house in one corner looked interesting. It was set back off the road and the garden had weeds and brambles everywhere. The little bungalow was a very sad sight; nothing had been touched for years and it needed a lot of attention.

As I walked passed the garage towards the bungalow an old lady came towards me. She was wearing a dirty old coat and her hair was all over the place and it had obviously not been washed for a long time. She had a small terrier dog with her on a long piece of rope. We got talking and I learnt that her name was Miss Hart. The outcome was that I offered to do some work cleaning up the garden and she would give me some pocket money in exchange. When I started on the back garden I was completely surprised at the size of it. Fruit trees were there but completely overgrown by brambles. I would spend weeks there in the school holidays and at weekends until it started to look like an orchard again.

We had no garage at our house, so one day I told dad that Miss Hart had an empty one. The outcome was that dad had a word with her and was able to rent it to store Geoff's motorbike there while he was away in the Navy. One weekend dad and I went round there to start the bike as Geoff was due home the following week. Dad had on his big brown duffle coat. He tried to kick start the bike but it refused to start.

Dad decided to put a bit of lighter fuel in the pipe and on the next try it started but flames leapt out all over the place. Dad told me to stand back and that it would stop in a minute. But it only got worse. I told dad to leave it as it may blow up. Dad took off his duffle coat and tried to smother the flames. He held it over the bike for quite a while and when he did take it off it was like something out of a comedy sketch. A Tommy Cooper one at that. There was a huge hole burnt through the coat. Poor dad's face was in panic mode. The fire was raging even more and was now under the seat and dad's much loved coat was trashed. I said I would go to the next house and get some water. I ran like hell, knocked on the door but got no reply. With that I picked up a bottle of milk off the doorstep and ran back. We threw the milk over the flames and the fire was put out.

Another time dad started the bike outside our house. It started up and took off with him running beside it until he could stop it, much to the amusement of my mates.

Geoff ran out of petrol late one night on his way home. He called dad who immediately left the house in his pyjamas with a coat over the top and drove to find him. He had the lighter fuel again. He put some in the bike. Geoff started the bike and was off. He was home and in bed by the time dad arrived back.

I can remember a horse drawn milk float in our road then years later I would help the milkman in his new motorised milk float. I also did a paper round. My first day was a disaster. I got in a right muddle and went home. Dad came out with me in the car. I was fine after that.

Dad and I used to visit the museums in London. He was always very good at taking me to interesting places. We would also go to the White City Stadium to watch the athletics. And often mum, dad and I would go to the London Palladium to watch one of the shows there. I can remember getting an autograph from Jimmy Edwards as he came out the stage door. Dad told the story about a lady at one of the shows laughing so much her false teeth flew out and rolled under the seats.

When Geoff was home on leave records would always be on the Dansette record player. Tracks like 'Diana' by Paul Anka 1957 and 'When' by the Kalin Twins 1958. 'The Great Pretender' by The Platters 1956 was a fabulous record. Neil Sedaka with 'Oh Carol' 1959. These were all tracks Geoff loved to play and I grew to like them too.

The first 78 record I bought was 'Be My Girl' by Jim Dale. It had a red centre if I am not mistaken. I went to a record shop under a bridge near Croydon to buy that record in 1957. I also loved Lonnie Donegan's 'Rock Island Line'.

At school I became friends with a boy whose father was a really well-known singer called Tony Brent. When his father collected him from our home he turned up in a magnificent white open top car with red leather seats looking every inch the star and he was always immaculately dressed. This was a bonus for mum as she really liked his records. He had quite a few hits from 1952 until 1959.

A couple of streets away lived a boy called Philip who had a hole in his heart. He was in a wheelchair and his complexion was very blue, but he loved to join in on all the pranks. I remember once throwing snowballs at our neighbour's back door. We could not push poor old Philip's wheelchair fast enough, so he was caught. "I've got him," shouted Jim Hopkins "The blue boy, he did it."

Go Karts were great fun and we were always playing about with them. We found a big hill to descend near Miss Hart's and nearly always came to grief at the bottom. It was near there that Charlie Drake the comedian stayed with a friend. I can remember knocking on the door and he signed an autograph for me.

By this time dad had invested in a TV. Small screen, about 9 inches, but dad bought this really powerful magnifying glass on a stand which stood in front. Shows like the Billy Cotton Band Show and Sunday Night at the London Palladium were on every week. Music was really starting to filter through to me more and more by now.

By the time I attended my last school, Hawes Down Secondary Modern School, I had progressed to having a new bass drum and snare. The kit was an Olympic in white. I also had a hi-hat. This was really it. I would shut myself away in my bedroom playing along to Joe Brown and The Shadows. I loved, and still do, 'Wonderful Land by' The Shadows. When Geoff was away for longer periods I would set my kit up in his bedroom as mine was very small. I did not have a drum tutor at this time and I was learning to play by myself.

Above: Paul on the drums

I can remember hearing 'Let There Be Drums' by Sandy Nelson in 1961. The sound of the drums was incredible. The reverb made them sound huge. Geoff had bought 'Happy Birthday Sweet Sixteen' and 'Breaking Up Is Hard To Do' by Neil Sedaka. I enjoyed those too.

Six Five Special was on the TV with all the up and coming stars. Some of whom I would get to work with later on. I liked Buddy Holly and The Crickets. Tony Meehan, the drummer with The Shadows, did a good solo track called 'See You in My Drums' on a Shadows' LP. He was a very sharp precise player. The front cover of the LP pictured The Shadows wearing bright coloured clothes which was very eye-catching and very cool. They were a class band. With Hank's distinctive guitar sound they were the band everyone was listening to.

I was very shy and would not let poor old dad come in to listen to me playing. I would make him stand outside the bedroom door to listen.

Hawes Down School was large and as well as the main building there were Portacabin classrooms. It was there where I bent down to push what I thought was a dead rat into the bushes not knowing that it had been poisoned and it bit me through the hand. I shook my hand but it was having none of it and sunk its teeth in further. I yelled to a friend to get it off. Needless to say I was back at the hospital again, this time for a jab. Poor mum nearly had a fit when the school rang to tell her I had been bitten by a rat and was at the hospital.

I never really liked this school and I did play truant a few times, getting my mate from across the road to write a note for me saying I had a bad cold. Mum was none the wiser as I kept out of the way from home and often hid in the loft of a house over the road when one of the boys was also playing truant. I can remember trying to hit the postman with a peashooter from there. One day we found an old bullet which we put in a vice and hit it with a nail and hammer. It went off ricocheting round the garage and it was a miracle that we were not hit.

This school was about 3 miles from home. I had always fancied a tandem bike, so one day dad bought me a second-hand one for £10. I would use it to cycle to school and pick up my friend Bernard Frost on the way. Bernard played guitar so we had a lot in common. Bernard got the nickname Sparrow. He was good at pulling faces and looking hurt when told off by the teacher.

We had woodwork classes and our teacher used to cook a fry up at lunchtime on one of the Bunsen burners in the classroom. One very foggy day we played a trick on him by hiding something then watched from outside the window. He came out after us with his frying pan containing half cooked eggs. We ran into the playing field so he could not see us through the thick fog. I could hear him shouting "I know it's you, Francis".

I had no interest in history because the teacher was not very friendly. I had the slipper from him several times. I also received the cane from the headmaster. On one occasion I put comics down the seat of my trousers. He smiled when he heard the sound of the cane on the books. I was told to take them out. I liked him as he was a fair man. He really did not want to cane anybody but had no choice as we had been sent to him. I must have deserved it, so I had no complaints.

When I was about thirteen whilst cycling to school one day I noticed a farm tucked back off the road. I stopped and admired the livestock. I went to the farmhouse and asked if they ever needed a hand at weekends. To my delight Mr. Cheeseman, the owner, said I could start on Saturday. He had a strong accent, always wore a flat cap, like the cartoon character Andy Capp, and had a roll-up cigarette hanging out the corner of his mouth.

I loved going to the farm. There were milking cows and calves. I was taught to milk 17 cows by machine and then there were 4 which had to be done by hand.

The amount of dung produced by the cows in the milking parlour was large. I was left to clear all that up while Mr. Cheeseman did other jobs. His two sons had no interest in the farm much to his dismay and he was glad of the help. His wife would cook us lunch and on occasions he would say there was a job there for me when I left school. The work was hard but fun. I enjoyed doing the haymaking and riding up on the hay being taken back to the barn. When the electric fencing was moved to a fresh area the power was left on. It was run by a battery but it gave a fair nip and took a bit of getting used to.

People often ask me what I would have done if I had not become a drummer. Well, most probably I would have been on a farm or worked with animals in some form or another. I was really getting into my music now and it was time to say goodbye to Cheeseman's farm.

Dad, Mum, Geoff, Paul
August 1960

Left: Paul and
Paul Norman

Chapter 2

The Takeovers, Astronauts, Chessmen, Rolf Harris and The Diggeroos, Bobby Sansom and The Giants, Bobby Christo and The Rebels

My first band when I was fourteen and a half had two guitarists (one rhythm and one lead) and myself. There was no bass player. Our first gig was on 9th June 1962 near Canterbury for a friend's son's wedding. I travelled down in my brother's motorbike sidecar with the drums in my lap and dad took the rest of the kit. We set up on the stage. We were called The Takeovers, however the man announcing us, said "Ladies and Gentlemen, please welcome The Potatoes". I was gutted. My first gig and the announcer got the name wrong. After the gig we stayed in a tent on the lawn and cooked baked beans. I thought I had made the Big Time!

The band used to rehearse at the home of one of the guitarists. He lived in a post war prefab home which was quite small. We mostly played instrumentals. I would also do the odd gig if a band needed a drummer and I did regular rehearsals with a big band. I loved the full sound of the brass. The players were much older than me but that made no difference as we all enjoyed the music.

Above: Geoff on the Ajax kit

The second band which I auditioned for were called The Astronauts. We mainly played in pubs and for payment someone at the end of the gig would go round the room with a hat for a collection. It was usually my dad. We would count the money and share it out. We did quite well and it was far more than boys at school were getting for pocket money. Around this time I bought my second drum kit which was a blue Ajax complete with two toms, a hi hat plus a crash ride cymbal. It felt so good to have a full kit at last.

It was almost guaranteed on a Saturday night gig at The Victory, Thornton Heath that a fight would break out. It usually started by all the glasses being swept off the bar. A bit like a scene in the saloon bar in a Western movie. The publican, who had a wooden leg like Long John Silver, would limp out from behind the bar and try to break things up. In the meantime dad would have jumped in front of the drum kit with arms outstretched so it did not get damaged.

We added a singer later on who called himself Rob Storm. He had his name written across the back of his jacket which made him look like a construction worker. At one of our gigs we played the Cliff Richard song Dynamite which was not Rob's best number. Dad was standing in the audience and as we finished the song a chap standing next to dad blew a raspberry. "The band's good, but the singer's rubbish" he informed dad. We had many laughs over that one.

Another funny occasion was at a pub called The Tigers Head in Catford when we were setting up. Dad saw a plug socket high up on a wall and he stood on a high stool to plug in our amps. There was an almighty bang and a flash. Poor dad had blown all the lights in the pub and had nearly fallen off the stool with shock. The funniest bit was dad trying to stay cool and ensuring everyone that everything was OK while the landlord was asking what the hell was going on!

9th JUNE WEDDING WITH DAVID HERN BAY –

" JUNE ROCK DANCE WITH THE STRANGERS. ESSEX.
£2.0.0

14th JULY WEDDING WITH DAVID TOTTENHAM 10/-

18th AUG PUB THORNTEN HEATH £1.11.6 (THE VICTORY)

30th AUG AUDITION BECKENHAM BALL ROOM.

31st AUG AUDITION GUILDFORD PLAZA BALLROOM.

SATURDAY 6th OCTOBER BLUE ANCHOR PUB, WEDDING
£1.10

1st SEP PUB VICTORY THORNTEN HEATH £1.5

15th SEP WEDDING BLAKE HALL £1.10

25th SEP THE TIGERS HEAD, AUDITION WITH THE
ORIGINAL CHECKMATES.

29th SEP PUB. THE KINGS HEAD. MITCHAM £1.5

4th Oct PLOUGH LANE 18/-
13th Oct the KINGS HEAD MITCHAM £1

Oct 14th AUDITION THE CASTLE TOOTING
OCT 20th Rock & TWIST FESTIVAL WITH THE PARTNERS
OCT 27th PUB THE VICTORY 28/-
THE HERCULES PUB 30/-
FRIDAY SATURDAY – SUNDAY AT THE VICTORY PUB £3.10

GOIN NEW GROUP THE CHESSMEN. PLAY AT
NEW NAME THE DIGGEROOS
ST MICHEALS HALL £2..0..0

TOUR FOR THE WEEKEND TO SCUNTHORPE AND
LUNETON. £3..10

=CHIOR SERVISE FOR THE CHURCH and A LITTLE ROCK
SESSON 10/-.

ST ANDREWS HALL CATFORD DANCE. MONEY SAVED FOR
THE TOUR WITH ROLF HARRIS.

START TOUR. FRIDAY 14th DECEMBER RITZ BALLROOM
#KINGS HEATH BIRMINGHAM, AND PLAZA BIRMINGHAM
THE Same night.

Saturday 15th December CARFAX Rooms, OXFORD
Sunday 16th December OASIS CLUB, MANCHESTER
TUESDAY 18th December IMPERIAL HALL WALTHAM X.
THURSDAY 20th December LYNDFORD CO CLUB THETFORD.
FRIDAY 21st December EBBISHAM, HALL EPSON
SATURDAY 22nd December WYKEHAM HALL
ROMPFORD £13.

Another time dad and I arrived at a large building where the band was rehearsing. Unfortunately it was on the fourth floor and there was no lift. As I was setting up the drums I could hear sirens wailing in the distance. They got louder and louder until they stopped right outside our building. I looked out of the window and to my horror the fire brigade were running in with hoses. That was the fastest dad and I evacuated a building. We ran like hell down the stairs with the drums to find the fire was on the ground floor. They were not aware anybody was in the building.

A couple of teachers at school found out about me playing and were very encouraging, which was nice. The only music lesson was 20 minutes singing, mainly hymns. Not what I wanted. So I went for private lessons at a music shop in Croydon. Doug, the owner of the shop was a small man who had one leg shorter than the other and he walked with a limp. He played upright double bass in a dance band with Joe the drum tutor. Joe was good on all the dance band things, but not the modern music. I started working there on a Saturday. When students wanted to learn the new rhythms the owner would say "You can teach them, Paul" and that was my early introduction at 14 years old to teaching. The name of Jeff Beck was mentioned by musicians coming into the shop as being a good guitarist to watch out for.

My next tutor was Ernie O'Malley from Croydon. He played in a Trad Jazz Band called the Clyde Valley Stompers and with Long John Baldry. Years later I heard a great story where Long John Baldry had been booked into a working men's club in the North of England. The compere announcing John onto the stage said "Ladies and Gentlemen, the next act I would not have booked but my daughter tells me he is very good. So here he is. Big Jack Bradley"

Ernie had also worked with many other well-known artists. I enjoyed these lessons and always looked forward to them each week eager to see what new patterns Ernie had to show me. Bernard was by now doing well on his guitar. We were always talking about music at school. Both of us could not wait to leave; we hated school.

The Shadows had a new drummer called Brian Bennett. He played a black pearl kit by Premier. Dad and I went to see them play and we thought he sounded great. He went on to play great tracks with The Shadows. I loved the track 'Rise and Fall of Flingel Blunt' and his drum solo track 'Little B'. These were classic tracks.

My next band was a big step for me. Dad would take me everywhere. In November I auditioned for a band called The Chessmen. They had a manager called George who had a good sense of humour. Most of the boys were older than me, in their twenties. They worked a lot and the equipment was good. They looked smart in matching waistcoats. To my surprise I got the job.

Previously on 25th September at The Tigers Head I had auditioned for The Original Checkmates, Emile Ford's ex backing band. The bass player told dad I was a good drummer but far too young to go on the road. So landing the job with The Chessmen was great. There was one big problem though. The band had been booked to do a package tour due to start in the following January, 1963. The tour would go all over England and we would be backing Rolf Harris. Rolf's hit song 'Sun Arise' was a track I liked very much. However I was just 15 years old and not due to leave school until the following July.

Mum thought I should get a trade behind me, but dad said this was a great opportunity for me, certainly too good to miss. So it was agreed that I should go with dad to talk to the headmaster at school. He was fantastic and said if that was what I really wanted to do then they would not stand in my way. To lose this opportunity for the sake of 6 months was pointless. I thanked him and he wished me luck. So out we walked. I was free at last.

Bernard was pleased for me. He went on to be a very successful songwriter, penning several hits for Status Quo. In fact many years later he saw an advert for one of my tuition videos and called me. We had in the meantime lost touch. He said when Status Quo needed a replacement drummer he told them he knew just the chap, but he could not find my number. By this time I had moved out of London to Essex. I am really pleased that he has done so well.

The gigs with The Chessmen went well. It was very exciting being on stage playing and meeting all the other bands. This was all pre-Beatles. Bands like Nero and The Gladiators and Screaming Lord Such and The Savages. We even backed Dickie Pride. He was a regular on the 6.5 Special TV show. He turned up about ten minutes before we went on. He said "Right, this is what I am doing tonight." He proceeded to explain each number in about 30 seconds and then on we went. Amazing; no rehearsal at all. The band was just winging it by the seat of our pants. But he was an amazing performer and vocalist. He seemed to make his whole body quiver which was unique. He was just one of many singers from that era who did not get the recognition they deserved, mainly due to bad management.

It was now full-on rehearsals. In January Rolf had several bookings for us to do which would help to get the band tight. We started rehearsing as a band and also with Rolf in a hall in Streatham. It was agreed that The Chessmen would change their name to The Diggeroos while on tour as this would be a good name to go with Rolf. We gigged as The Chessmen before starting the tour playing numbers by The Ventures, The Spotnicks and The Shadows with a few vocal numbers.

Above: The Diggeroos

On January 21st we were due to go to West Bromwich. For some reason we had no driver. I expect George was sick or away. Dad was asked if he could do it, so he took a day off work and drove the van. We were going along for quite a while when Rolf asked dad if he was going the right way. Dad said he thought so but Rolf said that we may be going back on ourselves and we had better stop and ask someone.

Dad pulled into a lay-by and walked back to where a bus had just pulled in. Dad stepped on to the bus to ask the conductor the way, but was trapped as more people got on. The bell went and so did the bus with dad still on board!   As it passed our van, Rolf said, "Here, Paul, was that your dad on that bus, I thought I saw him?"   We all looked as the bus went off up the road only to see dad leaping off a few hundred yards further on with his coat billowing out behind him.   We all fell about laughing.   Again it was just like a comedy sketch.   Frank Spencer; only years before.   But that gig was doubly doomed as we ran out of petrol on the way home.   Dad went off with a can to get some and Rolf sat with a scarf over his head reading a book.   Dad eventually got home at 5 a.m. and had the next day off work.

All my family including my Aunt Vera came to see one show with Rolf and I remember my bass drum beater going through the head.   That was embarrassing.   My brother Geoff came to the show at Edmonton on 24th January and he stood in the wings with Joe Brown watching our set.   Joe had not seen Rolf before and as he was due to tour with him he wanted to see what he was like.   Apparently he found it extremely funny and laughed all the way through!

On one gig the comedy duo Hope and Keen were also on the bill.   They asked me if I would stay on stage after our set and play some marching styles on the snare while they paraded around in khaki shorts and shirts.   It was very similar to "It Ain't Half Hot Mum".   They never offered me anything for my troubles, not even a drink, so I learnt a quick lesson there; but I did enjoy it and it was different.

I was in my element playing the drums and getting all this experience.   My tutor, Ernie, had asked me only a few months before whether I had thought about going professional.   I asked what that meant and he explained it was playing full-time and doing it for a living.   He said I was very good and should think about it.   So now it was all falling into place.

By now I was lodging in Brixton with George, his mum and sister.   This made it easier for me to be on hand for all the rehearsals and gigs.   Where we lived in Beckenham was a little too far away although dad was always there to help when he could.   No doubt my not being at home gave him a bit more time to himself.

The two main makes of vans used by bands were a Bedford Dormobile with sliding side doors or a Thames van.   The Thames van had the seats in the back facing each other with space in between and in the back for the equipment.   Often on the way to gigs with Rolf he would get his accordion out and I would set up the snare drum on a stand and we would have a play just to break the boredom of the journey.   Rolf was always great fun to be around.   If something was good one of his phrases was "fan bloody tastic".

The winter of 1962/63 was really bad with heavy snow and many roads were blocked. It was so bad that even the sea had frozen in places. The heater in the van was never very good and we were always cold. We constantly had to get out of the van to push a car that had got stuck, especially bubble cars which only had three wheels. Rolf always got out. "Come on lads" he would say "let's give them a push". In some places the snow was several feet deep. It was a nightmare to get to shows. We would collect Rolf from his house when he travelled with us. His wife, Alwen, was always very nice. Rolf carried a stage jacket and trousers on a coat hanger, plus the wobble board and the accordion.

The wobble board was great; I loved the sound plus the clave which Rolf played in Sun Arise. I remember someone saying to Rolf once that the drummer was a bit young. Rolf soon put him in his place. "He's good and does the job. What does it matter how old he is" was his reply.

It was time for the tour. On the bill were The Tornados, Joe Brown (whose records I had played along to in my bedroom only a year previously), Eden Kane, Marty Wilde and the Wildcats (who were only on the first two or three dates), Peter Jay and the Jaywalkers, Shane Fenton (later Alvin Stardust) and the Fentones, Jess Conrad, Susan Maughan, plus newcomers The Diggeroos, Peter Lodge, Mike and Tony Nevitt and from Canada Daryl Quist.

We would back all the new artists then Rolf, followed by Shane Fenton and the Fentones, with the Tornados closing the first half. They had just had a massive worldwide hit with Telstar which was No. 1 in the UK and America. Peter Jay and the Jaywalkers would open the second half followed by Jess Conrad, Susan Maughan and Eden Kane. Joe Brown and the Bruvvers would close the show.

The package tour of 39 dates kicked off on 15th February 1963 at Southend Odeon and finished on 31st March at the Liverpool Empire. A theatre I was to play at again later on with Tony Jackson. Larry Parnes was the tour promoter. The artists travelled in a coach but sometimes people would go alone. Joe travelled in his own transport. The Jaywalkers, Tornados and us were the main people every trip on the bus. We would all meet up in London in a small road next to Madam Tussauds. When we had a day off dad would collect me, usually about 3 o'clock in the morning and drive home. He would then drop me off back in London when we were leaving for the next show. It was always nice to get home.

The shows went well with good houses. I would stand in the wings and watch all the other acts. The Fentones had a good show. Peter Jay had coloured light bulbs in his drums so when he did his solo the stage lights were dimmed and one of the band members would stand in the wings and push the fader up as he hit each drum. Visually it was great.

ASTORIA, BRIXTON

Manager: W. F. Post

Telephone BRI 3452

TUES. MARCH 5th

6.30 and 9.00

ON THE STAGE

ONE NIGHT ONLY

LARRY PARNES PRESENTS

JOE BROWN AND THE 'BRUVVERS'

YOUR LUCKY STARS

SUSAN MAUGHAN

THE TORNADOS

EDEN KANE

JESS CONRAD
FILM PERSONALITY ✱

SHANE FENTON

ROLF HARRIS

PETER JAY AND THE JAYWALKERS

AL PAIGE

DARYL QUIST

The FENTONES

MIKE & TONY NEVITT

THE DIGGEROOS

PETER LODGE

Prices: 8/6   6/6   4/6

POSTAL BOOKING FORM—"YOUR LUCKY STARS"

Tuesday 5th March, 1963

To the Box Office, Astoria, Brixton

Date..................

Please forward.........................seats at.........................8/6 6/6 4/6 for the

evening 6.30/9.00 p.m. performance. I enclose stamped addressed envelope and P.O./Cheque value...............
(Please delete words not applicable)

NAME...........................

ADDRESS...........................

Your Lucky Stars

presented by Larry Parnes

☆☆☆☆☆☆☆☆☆☆☆☆☆☆☆☆☆☆☆☆☆☆

AL PAIGE introduces "New to You"

THE DIGGEROOS . PETER LODGE

MIKE and TONY NEVITT . DARYL QUIST

ROLF HARRIS

SHANE FENTON and the FENTONES

THE TORNADOS

interval

PETER JAY and the JAYWALKERS

JESS CONRAD

SUSAN MAUGHAN

EDEN KANE

JOE BROWN and the BRUVVERS

God Save the Queen

This programme is subject to alteration at the discretion of the Management

Tour Management and Administration	MARK FORSTER
Stage Director	PETER PANARIO
Stage Manager	EUAN FELTON

☆☆☆☆☆☆☆☆☆☆☆☆☆☆☆☆☆☆☆☆☆☆☆☆☆

Susan was very attractive and being the only lady always got a good reception from the audience. She was very easy going and would often chat in the wings waiting to go on. She had a big hit called Bobby's Girl. Eden Kane had hits which I enjoyed and I can remember hearing them on the juke box down the chalet. 'Well, I Ask You' was one I liked. Jess Conrad was the one the girls liked and was known for his acting on various TV shows and films. He had the looks and the personality though not exactly Little Richard vocal-wise.

I loved watching The Tornados. They were a good tight band. Clem Cattini, the drummer played great, and still does. Clem played a Trixon kit. Everyone loved Telstar when they played it. Our set was good fun. Peter Lodge was a nice chap; this was his first professional gig. Mike and Tony Nevitt were next, again no problem; they also went down OK. Daryl Quist was next. Off stage he came over a little flash for my liking, but pleasant enough. I wouldn't say he was the most popular person on the coach.

Below: Tour Programme

Peter Lodge

This tour marks the professional début into show business of Peter Lodge who, until recently, was a gentlemen's hair stylist. Born nineteen years ago in London, he is an avid record collector and enjoys reading and cycling. Given a live-audition in one of Larry Parnes' *Sunday Special* shows at Gt. Yarmouth last summer he received a great ovation.

Daryl Quist

Born in Ladysmith, Canada, just seventeen years ago, Daryl started learning to dance at the age of four and a year later entered show business by singing and dancing in shows. At the end of 1961 he came to Britain and got his first job here in the chorus of Tommy Steele's pantomime at Liverpool where he was seen by Larry Parnes, who put him into his summer show last year at Gt. Yarmouth. He has just made a record to be released early this year.

Mike & Tony Nevitt

Real brothers from Eastleigh, Hampshire, Mike and Tony started singing together five years ago and have since appeared in shows throughout the British Isles and have been seen regularly on Southern Television. Keen motorists and sports enthusiasts their ambition is to have a record at the top of the Hit Parade and to be good all-round entertainers.

The Diggeroos

Formed just six months ago at a youth club in Sydenham, London, the Diggeroos have already gathered a large following at ballrooms throughout the country where they have accompanied many recording artistes. Leader is Barry Tomlinson (*lead-guitar*), with Tony Key (*rhythm guitar*), Brian Nibbs (*bass*), and Paul Francis, at $15\frac{1}{2}$ is one of the youngest pro. drummers.

When I first started the tour I noticed that everyone was using eye liner and powder make up for their face. Someone said to try it as you need it to look better on stage. It also covered a white or spotty face. It did however cause a little fuss if we went into a pub before it had been washed off. We would often pop in when we had finished our set and were waiting for the other acts to go on. There was also an element of jealousy from the Rockers if their girlfriends were at the show. Often after the show while getting on the bus, the girls would be waiting outside with their boyfriends calling out from behind. If one got a bit close the coach driver would stand between him and the artists. Clem would also clear a path and give back as good as he got from the individual shouting out.

Doing Rolf's set was great. We would do one number on our own during the show. Rolf would do 'Tie Me Kangaroo Down Sport' and stretch the end out. He was great on the accordion. That song was a big hit for him in the UK. Then 'Sun Arise' followed a few years later. I loved playing 'Sun Arise'; big toms throughout the song. I remember going through two drum heads once while playing that number. I think I must have got carried away on that night.

BOOKINGS UP-TO-DATE

January	5th	White Hart, East Grinstead.
	12th	The Baths, Scunthorpe
	19th	Imperial Hall, Bletchley
	21st	West Bromwich
	24th	Edmonton
	25th	Haslemere
	26th	Lincoln
	28th	Solihul
	29th	Wallington
	31st	Swindon

FIRST TOUR

February	1st	Birmingham
	2nd	Bury St. Edmunds
	3rd	Southall
	4th	Pigalle, London

PACKAGE TOUR

February	15th	Southend Odeon
	16th	Tunbridge Wells Essoldo
	17th	Colston Hall, Bristol
	18th	Gaumont, Cheltenham
	19th	Gaumont, Worcester
	20th	Gaumont, Wolverahmpton
	21st	Essoldo, Stoke-on-Trent
	22nd	Gaumont, Derby
	23rd	Essoldo, Birkenhead
	24th	De Montford Hall, Leicester
	25th	Gaumont, Sheffield
	26th	Essoldo, Huddersfield
	27th	Odeon, Sunderland
	28th	Gaumont, Doncaster
March	1st	Odeon, Manchester
	2nd	Opera House, Blackpool
	3rd	Coventry Theatre
	4th	Gaumont, Watford
	5th	Astoria, Brixton
	6th	Odeon, Colchester
	8th	Gaumont, Ipswich
	9th	Theatre Royal, Norwich
	10th	Essoldo, Brighton
	11th	Gaumont, Rochester
	12th	Guild Hall, Portsmouth

March	13th	Odeon, St. Albans
	14th	Gaumont, Salisbury
	15th	Free
	16th	Winder Gardens, Bournemouth
	18th	Odeon, Guildford
	19th	Essoldo, Cannock
	20th	Odeon, Halifax
	23rd	Gaumont, Bradford
	24th	Hippodrome, Birmingham
	25th	Hippodrome, Stockton
	26th	Essoldo, Newcastle
	27th	Rialto, York
	28th	Gaumont, Southampton
	29th	Gaumont, Taunton
	31st	Empire, Liverpool

It was during that tour that I showed Rolf a copy of the Record Mirror showing Rolf's second single 'Johnny Day' had entered the chart, much to his delight. Over the years Rolf had many more hits. It always used to fascinate me to watch him sign an autograph. He would draw his head on a kangaroo's body then sign it. He is a brilliant artist. If anyone did heckle him on stage, God help them as he was so quick to make the person feel small with all the audience laughing at the heckler. You never heard another word from them.

Joe Brown and the Bruvvers were really good. Joe used to do the instrumental 'Hava Nagila', playing the guitar behind his head. He is a great musician who still tours and is very popular. A nice guy as well, very down to earth. It was a great thrill for me to be working with all these artists.

Rolf at 80 still entertained the crowds at Glastonbury and they loved him. People have grown up watching him on TV over the years; he has always been there and everyone knows him. What you see with Rolf is genuine. He has no big star attitude or ego. His paintings are fantastic. To be asked to paint the Queen was a great honour for him and shows the respect for his work. I look back at my time working with Rolf with fond memories. I cannot think of anyone better to work with for a 15 year old starting out in the music business.

I can remember one night we had finished our set and I was packing away my drums in the wings while Jess Conrad was performing. There was a metal rail at the top of the stairs leading to the stage. I had lent my cymbal against it. For some reason it twisted round and bounced down the stairs. It had a few rivets in it as well so the sound was really loud. Poor old Jess looked over as a few people in the audience started laughing. His manager came over to find out what was going on. It seemed to bounce on every step as it went down. Crash! Bang! Wallop!

The main artists stayed at hotels. We had to find bed and breakfast as we could not afford hotels every night. The B and B would cost about ten shillings. In some towns we had to share twin rooms if they were short of rooms. The tour was promoted by Larry Parnes, who had put quite a few of these tours together in the past. Al Paige was the compere for the night on this tour. He did a good job.

When I look at the dates of our tour now, I am amazed how many we did without a night off; sixteen in a row once. Nowadays there would be a night off every four or five shows. I usually did well at the bed and breakfast, being young the landladies always fed me up. They also enjoyed having us stay as it was a little different from their normal guests. Many were big fans of the artists on the show and would ask what they were like.

I was out of school and doing something I really loved plus meeting people and seeing different parts of England. Can't be bad! We would arrive at the theatre after lunch and get set up. We often did two shows in one night. If there was a matinee it would start about six thirty. We would try out new ideas or equipment at sound checks; anything to better the show. A number might be moved to a different position in the set to get a better impact on the night. We would also have to wash our own shirts and pants and try to dry them on radiators.

It was always sad when a tour finished as we were like one big family. At the end of the tour when we had been paid, Peter Lodge came into our dressing room looking very worried. He had had his money stolen. He had left it in his dressing room. We all had our suspicions who took the money. We had a whip round on the coach so he at least had some money to take home. The act of stealing is the lowest of the low especially from a fellow performer.

When the tour finished Clem arranged for me to meet him at Drum City in Charing Cross Road so I could invest in a new Trixon kit. He spoke to the owner and got me a good discount. The kit was bought on H.P. Mum said she would pay. I was over the moon. Poor old dad got 2 separate parking tickets as we were loading. The kit was blue and very smart. I still get excited to this day if I buy new drums. Clem really helped me and he is one of my oldest dearest friends. It is always lovely to catch up with him and his wife Ann. Clem is the one person who should write a book about his experiences as a musician. He has worked with just about everyone and played on over 42 number one hit records. An incredible achievement.

BEAT
MONTHLY
Popularity Poll

This poll is compiled every month from votes sent in by readers.

This Month		Last Month
1.	THE BEATLES	1.
2.	GERRY AND THE PACEMAKERS	3.
3.	THE SHADOWS	2.
4.	JET HARRIS AND TONY MEEHAN	4.
5.	BILLY J. KRAMER WITH THE DAKOTAS	5.
6.	THE JAYWALKERS	7.
7.	FREDDIE AND THE DREAMERS	8.
8.	THE TORNADOS	10.
9.	JOE BROWN AND THE BRUVVERS	9.
10.	THE ROLLING STONES	—
11.	THE SPRINGFIELDS	6.
12.	THE HOLLIES	15.
13.	DUANE EDDY	11.
14.	THE CRICKETS	14.
15.	THE EAGLES	19.
16.	THE BIG 3	13.
17.	SOUNDS INCORPORATED	12.
18.	THE OUTLAWS	—
19.	THE DIGGEROOS	16.
20.	THE SPOTNICKS	

Don't forget to vote for your TWO favourite G & I stars by writing their names on a postcard and sending it to: Beat Monthly Pop Poll, 244 Edgware Road, London, W.2. REMEMBER . . . YOUR vote is important.

We played one more big show with Rolf at the Victoria Palace on Sunday 5th May 1963. This was for the Songwriters Guild and was held most years. Acker Bilk and his Paramount Jazz Band were playing plus Kenny Lynch and the Viscounts, Mrs. Mills and Jackie Trent whose husband Drew Harvey we backed on a few occasions. Maureen Evans was also there and Alan Freeman, plus good old George Chisholm and Ann Shelton.

After the tour work was very thin on the ground at times so The Chessmen backed a girl singer who was more cabaret really. Later on we added Lance, a male vocalist, to the band to see if that would help. While on the tour we were amazed to find out that in Beat Instrumental magazine we had been voted into the top twenty bands at number 16 alongside our heroes The Shadows and other top bands of that time. That was a great thrill but alas it did not help work matters. By then Tony the guitarist had left and been replaced by Clive. I took a few weeks' work at a plastics factory in Brixton just to pay the rent. It was a small family run business called Harmans.

Eventually I could see the band was going to fold as members were getting restless. Barry was a good guitarist so he was getting itchy feet. By this time mum and dad had moved to 25 Cress Way, Faversham, a small town in Kent and I moved back home until I could find another band. I used to go to the local coffee shop and play the new records on the juke box.

London City Agency Handout

Photograph includes drummer Paul Francis, second from front, who played with The Giants for two months at the beginning of 1964. Paul left the band because at sixteen years of age he was unable to get a work permit for Hamburg, Germany.

Paul later joined up with ex-Searchers bass player Tony Jackson and the Vibrations.

BOBBY SANSOM and the GIANTS

One day in October 1963 I bought a magazine and saw an advert for a drummer in Hove, Brighton. It was for a band called Bobby Sansom and The Giants. I went down for the audition and got the job. Apart from Bobby the singer, there was Trevor Duplock and Bill Smith on guitar and Mick Grinwade the bass player. As I did not live locally Mick said I could lodge with him and his parents. It was a big

Bobby Sansom and the Giants in the famous Liverpool Cavern

house with large rooms. Mick and I got on fine, but again everyone was older than me.

We had quite a lot of work and we even played at the famous Cavern Club in Liverpool in February 1964. The band was offered work at The Star-Club in Hamburg, Germany in March but they were going to turn it down as I was underage.

I told them to take it and I would look for something else so I left them the beginning of March. Germany had very strict laws for people under 18 working after 10 p.m.

So I was home again, checking all the adverts for Drummer Wanted. My next band was called Bobby Christo and The Rebels. This time apart from Bobby who was a little older, most of us were the same age. Denis Thompson played rhythm guitar, John Herve on lead, Kenny Rowe on bass. Later on Denis took over on bass when Kenny left. They already had a single out on Decca records. We all got on very well. I remember at one gig the place was not earthed and Kenny got an electric shock when he touched his mic and guitar at the same time. The smell of burning flesh was horrible. Denis quickly took off his guitar and kicked the mic stand out of Kenny's hand and probably saved his life. Kenny had an awful scar.

HEAR A HAUNTING BALLAD ON
"THE OTHER SIDE OF THE TRACK"
BY
BOBBY CRISTO
AND THE REBELS
on DECCA F 11913
Sole Agency : ADEN ENTERTAINMENTS
SEDLEY HOUSE, LOUGHTON, ESSEX
Telephone : LOUGHTON 2559

38

BOBBY CRISTO AND THE REBELS	DECCA

From the hard training ground of playing in London pubs come Bobby Cristo and The Rebels. They owe their present success to their manager, Joe Carolan. Joe had, in fact, played in a "pop" group before the war caused it to break up. After the war he became a civil engineer and as his business flourished, he decided to find a group of his own.

The first place he went to was the East End of London where he scouted clubs and pubs for talent and talented boys he found, but not all in the same group. Each of them came from a different group and together Joe formed them into Bobby Cristo and The Rebels.

Between them they have a wealth of experience, earned by several years' playing in other groups, both here and abroad.

.... BOBBY has been singing for three years and has been to Germany with another group.

.... PAUL FRANCIS has played the drums since he was eleven and has backed people like Rolf Harris and Bobby Samson, although still only 17.

.... KENNETH RQWE, bass guitarist, has been playing for two years with other groups. He, besides playing his instruments, makes them himself.

.... DENNIS THOMPSON has been playing harmonica/rhythm guitar for two years with amateur groups.

.... JOHN HERVE, lead guitarist, has played the guitar since he can remember.

We would travel around in a Dormobile. Half the time people had to sit on the equipment in the back. The front had two passenger seats and the driver's seat. The band was based in Barking, Essex. I found lodgings there. One room. The landlady told me "Don't worry what time you get up, your breakfast will be ready." You're telling me it would be ready! Egg and bacon cooked the night before and left on the table with a plate over the top. The fat had glued it to the plate! It is not a dish I could recommend cold. Perhaps that is why she put a plate over the top; maybe she could not stand the sight of it. I ate it but hated it.

When Denis told the story to his mum and sister they said tell Paul he can stay here. Denis had two beds in his room and I could have one of them. Thank Heaven; I was saved from another day of that dreadful food. I had put up with it for a few weeks. Denis and his parents, Grace and Tom and his sister Pat made me so welcome.

Another local band was Brian Poole and The Tremeloes. They were having hit records. The Symbols were another good local band as were Tony Rivers and The Castaways. Denis used to play in a band with Steve Marriott, John Herve, Colin Green and a drummer called Tony McIntyre. It was called Steve Marriott and The Frantiks, later to be The Moments. John and Denis quit to join The Rebels. At one point Steve stayed with Denis and his family for several months after falling out with his parents. The Thompson family always had an open door.

Tony McIntyre was a good player and great fun to be around, always laughing and joking. Steve and Tony used to come round to 78 Netherfield Gardens, Barking, to visit Denis and me. One night Denis, Steve and I went to see a band. Steve wandered off and the next thing we saw him on stage singing and playing harmonica. His voice just blew me away, so powerful and great harp playing to match. This was the first time I had heard him sing. Steve was only small and you would never expect a voice like that to come out of such a slight frame. I would often call in at his flat which he shared with his mum, dad and sister. Steve would play all this blues stuff to me, Sonny Boy Williamson and Muddy Waters.

Steve was a child actor who had played a part on stage in Oliver Twist. As he got older he chose music instead of acting. He was always very confident and sure of what he wanted to do. Some years later when I was doing well with Tony Jackson I gave him my jacket which he liked and I paid for Tony McIntyre's taxi fare when he came over to see us. I enjoyed their company. Steve went on to huge success with The Small Faces then Humble Pie with Peter Frampton. Sadly he died in a fire at his house in 1991, such a tragic loss. He had one of the best voices in the business, along with Stevie Winwood and Chris Farlowe. Great soulful voices. Steve was also a good showman and guitarist.

Denis's father, Tom, was a nice man and he would often give us money if we were a bit short. He had a good job at Ford Motors. Gracie, his wife was lovely. She was like a mother hen keeping us all in check. Patrica, their daughter, was like a sister to me. Like Gracie she was always looking after Denis and me. We all got on so well. Denis and I were always playing pranks on Pat. If she brought a boyfriend home it would be eggs thrown to each other while the hapless boyfriend looked on in horror waiting for one to break!

Most gigs were local. There was the odd time that we would travel further. One gig was on the Isle of Wight. We had no money for a hotel so we slept on the beach. We put deckchairs all round and on top making a hut. A policeman popped his head in to ask what was going on. After we had explained our situation, he said it was OK for us to stay but to make sure we put the deckchairs back in the morning.

Occasionally a friend called Mike who liked the band would do the driving for us and help set up the equipment. Our very own roadie! This was always very welcome. Driving back after a gig can be dangerous if you are tired. Mike did a great job.

At one point Denis and I helped out a local band called The Syndicats. They played mainly R & B. The guitarist was Steve Howe who later played with Yes. We would pick him up from his house on our way to gigs or rehearsals.

On one occasion we were travelling home from a gig in the early hours of the morning when we had a slight accident. There was a lady manager as well as the band members in the van. The driver misjudged a corner and we struck a bridge on our left. The driver put on the brakes, the van doors flew open and the back seat, which had not been bolted to the floor, did a somersault with me and other band members going with it right out into the road. It was like The Keystone Cops! We were alright, just shaken. The lady in front cut her face.

The noise from the vehicle scraping down the metal bridge brought out a man from his house. He was wearing a pair of trousers and a vest and had been shaving. One side of his face was shaven while the other was covered with shaving foam. It was very comical. He was quite concerned that we were alright. Luckily apart from a few cuts and bruises we were.

THE DIGGEROOS

Account since W.Brom:

Expenses:

Van Hire:

Edmonton	£ 2. 0. 0
Haslemere	£ 2. 0. 0
Lincoln	£ 2. 0. 0
Wallington	£ 2. 0. 0
Swindon	£ 2. 0. 0
Birmingham	£ 2. 0. 0
Birmingham	£ 2. 0. 0
Southall	£ 2. 0. 0
	£16. 0. 0

Petrol :

Fill up: W.Brom	£ 1.14. 3
Haslemere	£ 1. 8. 0
Lincoln	£ 1. 6. 6
Lincoln	£ 1.17. 6
Fill up Lincoln	£ 1. 4. 4
Fill up Wallington	£ 16. 0
Swindon	£ 1. 4. 7
Swindon	17. 6
Birmingham	£ 1. 9. 3
Birmingham	£ 1. 6. 6
Birmingham	£ 17. 8
Birmingham	£ 17. 4
Fill up Southal	£ 1. 9. 6
	£16. 8.11

Sundries:

Jackets	£ 32. 0. 0
Bow Ties	£ 1.14. 0
Strings	17. 6
Mr. Key	10. 0
Make up	£ 1.11. 8
Clothes Hanger	11. 6
Cafe Brum	10. 0
Guest House	5. 5. 0
Manager's fares in Taxies.	3. 5. 0
	£46. 4. 8

Salaries:

Manager's @ 15%	£ 30. 0. 0
Barry Tomlinson	£ 23.10. 0
Tony Key	£ 23.10. 0
Brian Nebbs	£ 23.10. 0
Paul Francis	£ 25.10. 0
	£126. 0. 0

Grand Total   £204.13. 7

Receipts:

Agency	£200. 0. 0		
Balance last Acc.	£ 8. 2. 7	£218.2.7 Bal.	£ 13.15. 0d
Deposit Gar.Ret.	£ 10. 0. 0		

Left: The Diggeroos with new guitarist Clive

Chapter 3

Tony Jackson and The Vibrations

The sixties was a fantastic time for music. Once The Beatles had burst onto the scene it opened the doors for so many more artists. It was a very exciting time. Bands were appearing from all parts of the country; many with a different individual sound. The Animals had a totally different sound from say The Beatles, The Rolling Stones or The Searchers.

We would often support named bands which drew the audiences, which was good for us as it meant we were getting exposure. On separate occasions we supported The Rolling Stones and The Merseybeats at Club Noreik, Tottenham. Things were going alright for the band, but not exactly taking off. One day in July 1964 I read in a paper that Tony Jackson the lead singer and bass player with The Searchers was quitting the band. It was very big news. The Searchers at that time were a huge band. Very popular. They had clocked up five big hits: three number one hits, one number two and one number eleven.

Tony sang lead on 'Sweets for My Sweet' and 'Sugar and Spice'. Mike Pender, the guitarist, took lead vocals on 'Needles and Pins', 'Don't Throw Your Love Away' and 'Someday We're Gonna Love Again'. Chris Curtis the drummer did harmonies. John McNally played rhythm guitar and did backing vocals on their first LP. Tony sang lead on tracks like 'Farmer John', 'Ain't Gonna Kiss You No More', and 'Love Potion Number Nine'. All were classic tracks that had also been released on an EP which made the charts. They were big hits in America for the band. The reason for Tony leaving was put down to musical differences. Tony's voice was very distinctive. There was no mistaking it for anyone else.

A couple of months after leaving the band, Tony went into hospital to have plastic surgery on his nose. Again this was big news in the papers. He had said he always wanted a smaller nose and the bump taken out. So he now had the time and money to do it. The article also said he would be putting a new band together and Tito Burns who handled The Searchers would also represent Tony. The article also mentioned which hospital Tony was in.

Right, I thought, I will write to him and offer him my services, never thinking for one minute that I would hear anything back. About a week later I was gob smacked to receive a letter back from Tony asking me to call Tito Burns' office and arrange an audition.   I was so excited, but I realised there was a long way to go yet.   I told Denis who was pleased but also worried as I may leave the band.

I called Tito's office and they said auditions were being held at The Roaring Twenties Club in London and told me to be there at a certain time.   A drum kit would be provided. Tony was also looking for a guitarist and a keyboard player; all the equipment for them was also provided.   Denis came along to give me support.   There was a hold up getting into the club but eventually the doors were opened.   It was about 2 o'clock in the afternoon so it was only being used for auditions.   The club was full with over a hundred musicians.   I'm thinking, "Boy! Have I got my work cut out here!" as a third of the people there were drummers.

Tony arrived a little later and sat down at a table along with two other men.   They had note pads in front of them, a bit like the X Factor judges.   All the musical equipment was set up down one end, drums, amps and keyboards.   One of the gentlemen called out my name and asked me to take my place on the drums and to play along to a track.   The track was by a group from Liverpool called The Undertakers. "Hells Bells" I thought, "I'm first on, all eyes are on me, I'd better get this right or I will be the one being buried!"

When the track finished, a guitarist called Ian Buisel was called up, followed by a keyboard player who was also called Paul.   He was Paul Raymond.   The gentleman then asked us to have a play so they could see how we worked together.   It seemed to work OK.   "Thank you" the gentleman said.   I sat down with Denis and watched various other combinations always starting with the drummer playing to the track on his own. Quite a few players were struggling saying they could not hear the track well enough.   I think some of them were just too loud; it sounded like they were trying to build a shed!

There were some good players there and it was interesting watching them all.   At least I had finished, that was the good thing about going first. The drummers that followed did have the edge by having now heard the play along track.

After about an hour I was thinking this is going to take hours.   I told Denis that I thought we should go.   We walked over to the table where Tony and the two gentlemen were sitting and I said that I would be leaving.   The gentleman said "No, don't go, you've got the job.   It is just a formality hearing the others."   I could not believe what I was hearing.   I had got the job!   Tony asked me to wait so that we could talk.   Denis and I sat down again.   As the others played I was not really listening now as Denis and I talked.   He needed a new drummer for his group and I asked if there was anyone there that he liked.   We both agreed on one chap called John.

44

At the end Tony thanked everyone for coming and announced that he had chosen me, Ian and Paul. Denis then spoke to John who was disappointed not to get the job with Tony but was interested in joining the Rebels. At least this would save Denis and the boys the trouble of advertising and auditions.

As the various musicians made their way out, Ian, Paul and I had a quick chat. They were both gob smacked as well. Tony came over and said that we needed to go to Tito Burn's office. We left Denis chatting with John, went upstairs and Tony hailed a taxi. We all piled in. On the journey I could not help thinking that this all seemed so unreal.

We arrived at the office at the top of a large building. Very plush with nice carpets. The receptionist asked us to take a seat and Mr. Burns would not be very long. Eventually we were told we could go in. Tony introduced us one by one to Tito. A man who reminded me of Sam Costa in looks with his white moustache. He was very pleasant and invited us all to sit down. He asked if any of us had any problems about working full-time with Tony and if we had any commitments elsewhere. "No" was the unanimous reply. "Right", he said "You are in the studio next week to cut your first single for Pye records. Tony Hatch will be the A and R man; he produced The Searchers. We have three TV shows booked and radio shows to do. On 19th September you start a 29 day tour with The Hollies and Freddie and The Dreamers."

It was all starting to move so fast; TV shows and he had not even recorded the single yet! Now, money-wise it was agreed we would receive forty five pounds a week whether we worked or not. Tito wanted to make it less, but Tony said no, they must have forty five. I think Tony really wanted about sixty, anyway forty five pounds a week was more than my dad was earning. I had no complaints, having nothing it was a fortune for me. It was arranged that every week we would come to the office to collect it.

SUNDAY MIRROR. September 13, 1964

PICTURED TOGETHER for the first time—Tony Jackson with his own group, The Vibrations. Tony, previously lead singer with The Searchers, struck out on his own after a disagreement over policy. "I found the soft, sweet approach of The Searchers too watery," he said. "I prefer the gutsy, strong beat we followed in the early days, back home in Liverpool." That's what Tony goes after on his first disc, Bye, Bye, Baby and Watch Your Step, released by Pye on Tuesday. He chose The Vibrations after auditioning 400 aspiring pop stars—and has spent nearly £3,000 of his own money backing his hunch.

I left Tito's still not quite believing what had happened. When I got home I sat down and talked about it with Denis and the family. They were all very pleased for me which was nice.

45

IT'S surprising what something like a new nose can do for someone. Tony Jackson has never liked his nose.

"It was horrible. It was giving me a complex," he says. He was always saying that he came out wrong in photos. It really worried him and got him down.

But, what with his breaking away from the Searchers, and looking out for a new group, Tony found he had time on his hands. Time enough to have his nose changed, and that's something he's always wanted to do.

And now? Well, personally, we've never seen such a happy, lively Tony before. It's made all the difference in the world to him and his face.

But after the operation, it was back to looking for a new backing group. Tony wanted a group that could produce an earthy wild sound, featuring the organ a lot—as shown in his first great disc "Bye Bye Baby".

"Well, after hundreds of auditions at the Roaring Twenties Club, we finally came up with Martin Raymond on organ, Ian Buisel on lead and rhythm and Paul Francis on drums." Tony, of course, being the bass guitarist and lead vocalist.

Tony is now really in his element. He can say exactly what songs he thinks they should do, and keeps the boys on their toes as to appearances, because as far as the Vibrations are concerned, Tony is an old hand, showing them the ropes.

"I'm glad, anyway," said Tony, "that at least we don't have to start at the bottom of the ladder. All the ground work has been done before by me!" Judging by the receptions they got on the Freddie/Hollies tour, it won't be long before Tony's up at the top of the ladder once again!

NEWS ABOUT THE NOSE

We went to a tailor and had blue suits made for stage. Tony bought a van for us all to travel in and we had a road manager called Malcolm to drive us and help set up. This van was second-hand and kept breaking down so Tony eventually had to buy a new one. This was all a far cry from what I had been used to. This was all so well organised. We were to do the TV show Ready, Steady, Go! on September 11th, followed by Thank Your Lucky Stars on the 12th plus BBC 2's Open House on the 26th followed by Top of The Pops on 22nd October. These were big shows which I would always watch when I could. We agreed a date to start rehearsing at Tony's flat in Kensington. We also met there and had some photos taken for the press.

The following week I arrived at Pye Studios at Marble Arch. I really liked it there. It had a good vibe about the place. There were big photos of the stars on the wall going down the stairs to the studio. There were always other people about in one

studio while we were recording in another. We had the big studio booked for our session. Tony introduced us to Tony Hatch who was very nice and made us all feel welcome. Our main object was to cut the A and B side. We had two songs, 'Bye, Bye Baby' which was an old Mary Wells track, plus a Bobby Parker track called 'Watch Your Step'.

I set up my Trixon kit and once we were all ready we had a little jam. Then Tony Hatch did individual sound checks. Now we were ready. We had been rehearsing these two tracks at Tony's flat, much to the annoyance of his neighbours who would often complain.

Top: Paul rehearsing in Tony's flat

Right: PYE Studios September 1964. Tony, Paul, Tony Hatch, Ian, Martin

The session went very well. We all played well and had the two tracks down quite quickly which I think surprised Tony Hatch. In one section in 'Bye, Bye Baby', I gave the track a double time feel just for one bar which worked well. Tony was really pleased with all of us. The Breakaways vocal group were hired to do backing vocals. The three ladies had built up quite a reputation of being very good in the studio; they had good voices. One of them, Vicki, went on to marry Joe Brown. Their daughter, Sam, has done well in her own right as a singer.

LOOKING FOR EXCITEMENT

L. to R.—IAN BUISEL (Lead Guitar)   MARTIN RAYMOND (Organ)   TONY JACKSON (Bass Guitar)   PAUL FRANCIS (Drums)

TONY JACKSON and The Vibrations have been getting down to the job of building up their repertoire.

I dropped in to see them rehearsing the other day, and when they stopped for a cup of tea, I asked Tony what were his aims for the new outfit.

"Excitement," he answered right away, "We don't want people to sit back and relax when we're on and say 'How Nice.' We want them to be up on their feet dancing, even if they're in a theatre. Pretty songs are O.K. for records but if people see you live they want to be shaken."

The boys who Tony picked to help him shake the people are Paul Francis, who plays drums; Martin Raymond, organist; and Ian Buisel, lead guitarist.

I chatted to Ian next. I noticed, while he was practising, that he had a very fast action and asked how he had worked it up. "Oh, that's not all me," he said modestly, "the great action on this Gibson of mine helps a lot." He picked up his guitar and fingered it lovingly. "It's one of the old models," he went on, "a Les Paul Special. I much prefer them to the new double cut-aways. The sound is fantastic. I've had this one three years and it's still as good as new. You can't get them now. I use a Vox A.C. 30 with it and it really screams even above the organ and Tony's bass."

"Yes," said Tony, "you need extra volume with old Martin here, once he gets going you have to prise him away from those keys." Martin looked hurt. "What about you with your monstrous, great Epiphone?" he replied. "Ah," said Tony, "You know very well I'm a blender more than a dominator."

No, the Vibrations weren't falling out. Friendly banter is just a part of their very good working relationship which is, in fact, one of the best I've seen.

Later Tony told me that he was very pleased with the new set-up. "The boys are all great musicians," he told me, "and they're picking-up the new numbers very fast."

Tea finished, they got down to work again and ran through "What Did I Say," "Love Potion Number Nine," and tried out Little Richard's "I Can't Believe You Wanna Leave," searchin' for that extra-special excitement all the time.

Tony and the girls put the vocals down with Ian and Paul doing backing vocals as well. By now Paul was using his middle name of Martin so not to confuse people with two Pauls. My dad had not given me a middle name as he said it was always a nuisance filling in forms if you have several names. So Paul was now Martin Raymond. I do not think he liked it but it was what Tony wanted, so he agreed.

Hearing everything finished sounded fantastic. I felt so pleased for Tony and he was chuffed to bits. We had some press photos taken in the studio. I think it all hit home a week later when I bought a copy of Record Mirror music paper and there was our photo staring out at me. That was the moment I realised I had joined Tony Jackson.

Only a year before I had bought The Searchers LP and now I was in a band with Tony. The group was called The Vibrations. Tony did not want to use his name but Tito said he must as it would help sales. So the band became Tony Jackson and The Vibrations. A little while later our picture was in The Sunday Mirror and many other magazines.

RECORD MIRROR, Week ending September 4, 1964

FIRST record by ex-Searcher **Tony Jackson's** new group, **The Vibrations,** is the **Mary Wells'** number, "Bye Bye Baby." Tony and his three-man group recorded it at Pye's London studios last Wednesday. Flip is an old number recorded by **Bobby Parker** in America, "Watch Your Step."

The disc will be released on Friday, September 18. Pye had planned to record Tony this week, but the group stepped in when, ironically, The Searchers could not use the studios as planned, because of the illness of Mike Pender.

A & R man Tony Hatch told RM's Barry May after the session: "We've gone all out on this record to get away from the conventional group sound. I wanted something different, and we've treated the number as an arrangement, with The Breakaways vocalising as well." The group recorded two other titles, which may be used on their second single release.

Published here is the first picture of Tony Jackson and the Vibrations, taken at the recording session.

Left to right are **Tony** (bass guitar and lead vocal), **Paul Francis** (17, drummer, of Barking), **Ian Buisel** (20, lead guitarist, of Wallington), and **Martin Raymond** (18, organist, of Kensington).

The group has been booked for Ready, Steady, Go, next Friday, September 11.

It was a great feeling to buy a paper and see the band in there. 'Bye, Bye Baby' was chosen for the A-side with 'Watch Your Step' as the B-side. Once we had finished recording we started rehearsing again for live shows. We were booked to do a few dates before the tour started. It was not unusual to do two shows in one night at separate venues. The second could be twenty miles away. We only did a twenty minute spot if we had two shows. It was hardly time to get warmed up. Poor Malcolm, our road manager, was always kept on his toes. Ian and I would help to set up if we were in a rush.

Martin was never too keen. He got the nickname Hands as he did not like to get his hands dirty. He had a good sense of humour and he and I were always laughing about something. Ian's hair was pushed back so he was given the nickname Rocka. Because I was tall and thin I became Twizzle or Twiz.

New to the Charts

Tony's new approach pays off

CONFESSED Tony Jackson, when told of his chart success with "Bye Bye Baby": "Phew! That's a load off my mind. I was hoping and praying it would get into the NME Top 30. I didn't set my sights too high—just to get in the chart would be enough."

So it's welcome to the charts for Tony under his own name and with his own group, the Vibrations (above). Although, of course, with the Searchers Tony was no stranger to the charts.

The weeks between leaving the Searchers and getting his new record out, have been anxious ones. "That's natural," he told me. "It was a big step I took leaving the Searchers—but it was

a step I had to take for many reasons.

"One of them was my particular liking for the more robust type of beat music, rhythm 'n' bluesy sounds. That's why I chose 'Bye Bye Baby' for our first record: it was written by Mary Wells and I like her kind of singing."

But if the past few weeks have been anxious ones for Tony, he had a lot of things to cheer him up. He says: "I was surprised and delighted at the amount of fan mail I received. It gave me a tremendous uplift at a time I needed it."

So that's Tony Jackson—a new nose, a new group, a new approach . . . and a new hit! I.D.

RECORD OF THE WEEK

Tony Jackson And The Vibrations

BYE BYE BABY 7N 156

Adam Faith and The Roulettes, Cliff Bennett and The Rebel Rousers and Bill Haley and The Comets were on Ready Steady Go with us on 11th September. We did two or three TV shows with Bill Haley and The Comets. I got on very well with their drummer. 'Rock Around The Clock' and 'Shake, Rattle and Roll' were tracks that everybody knew and loved.

On 3rd October 1964 'Bye, Bye Baby' came in at number 30 in the NME (New Musical Express) chart and number 19 in Teen Beat. It was a fantastic thrill. It finished up at number 25, and 38 in Record Mirror. My first ever recording and it was a hit. I could not believe my luck. I remember walking down a street one day and all I could see from

TONY JACKSON COULD HAVE A HIT

Friday, September 18, 19..

CAN Tony Jackson get himself the same kind of success the Searchers have, now he is an ex-Searcher? I think he can with "Bye Bye Baby," a tune written by Mary Wells.

Backed by the Vibrations, it is an up-tempo with Tony dual tracking away over a pounding beat. The approach is a lot more raw'n'beaty than the Searchers, although Tony retains occasional touches from his former group.

"Watch Your Step" is on the B side of this Pye release and it features an r-and-b organ playing simple riffs before Tony (again double tracks) comes in and whips himself into a fair state of excitement.

TONY JACKSON (third left) and his VIBRATIONS.

ABOUT PAUL

Can you tell me anything about the drummer with The Vibrations, Tony Jackson's group?—Gillian Brookes (Stoke Newington).

Drummer Paul Francis was born in Beckenham, Kent, on 11th October, 1947. He now lives in Barking. He attended the Horsedown Secondary School, and left at 15. He played with a number of local groups before joining The Vibrations. Paul has a brother, Geoff, who is in the navy.

Big time

TONY JACKSON and the Vibrations should head straight into the big-time, to judge from their debut on ABC-TV's "Lucky Stars".

One cannot, of course, pass a proper judgment on a group on one mimed show, but their personality came across and turned an average sort of record into a good performance. — B.D.

Ex-Searcher for TV

EX-SEARCHER Tony Jackson and his new group, the Vibrations, is set for his TV debut.

It will be on Rediffusion's "Ready, steady, go!" on September 11. The following weekend (19) Jackson televises on "Lucky stars".

Tony's quartet comprises himself on bass guitar, Martin Raymond, 18-year-old organist from Kensington, London; lead guitarist Ian Buisel, aged 21 from Wallington, Surrey, and 17-year-old Barking drummer Paul Francis.

The Jackson group's debut single—"Bye bye baby"—will be released on September 18.

TONY LEAVES HOSPITAL

Tony Jackson, former bass guitarist with The Searchers, was expected to leave the London Clinic on Monday evening after a plastic surgery operation to straighten his nose. Whilst in hospital, Tony has been sorting through the hundreds of letters fans have sent him via the Record Mirror, suggesting names for his new group, as yet, still unformed.

TONY'S NEW GROUP

Former member of THE SEARCHERS, TONY JACKSON, pictured at B.B.C. TV's "Top of the Pop" studios in Manchester last week with his new group, THE VIBRATIONS.

Tony was there to promote his disc "Bye Bye Baby," which entered the Top Thirty charts.

Jackson records his debut disc

FORMER Searcher Tony Jackson has himself produced his first record for Pye with his new group, the Vibrations. He cut several tracks for his manager Tito Burns', Lindon Records, aided by Pye recording manager, Tony Hatch.

Titles for the first single have not yet been selected but release date is set for September 18.

In conjunction with the record release, Jackson will appear on Rediffusion's "Ready, Steady, Go!" (September 11), ABC-TV's "Lucky Stars Summer Spin" (19th), and BBC-2's "Open House" (26th).

TONY JACKSON ON FREDDIE'S SHOW

FORMER Searcher Tony Jackson and his new group, together with chart newcomer Julie Rogers, have been added to the Freddie and the Dreamers one-nighter tour which opens at Slough Adelphi on September 19.

As previously reported, the Four Pennies and the Hollies are also set for the tour which runs until October 18.

Freddie and the Dreamers are to play two weeks in variety in November.

They play November 9 week at Nottingham Theatre Royal, and the following week at a venue still to be set.

Tony Jackson and The Vibrations

Bye Bye Baby; Watch Your Step
(Pye N 15685) ★★★

EX-SEARCHER Jackson's debut with his new group is a brisk one and should register happily with customers. Girl group is also brought into play for some vocal accompaniment as Tony chants Bye Bye Baby. Baby may sleep.

Turnover's faster with more emphasis on the instrumental noise, and the organ sound will catch a few ears.

Complete with new nose, new group and a new sound, Tony Jackson is back in Glasgow with his own group the Vibrations

EX-SEARCHER Tony Jackson had this week "nearly arrived at the line-up" for his new Combo.

Tony, who entered a London hospital last week to have an operation on his nose, is now out—with what a friend of Jackson's describes as "a less conspicuous nose".

Jackson and his new Combo makes its debut at Slough Odeon on September 19, at the start of an extensive tour topped by Freddie and the Dreamers.

Searchers join Jackson on TV

THE Searchers will now appear on ABC-TV's "Thank Your Lucky Stars" on the same day (19th) as ex-member Tony Jackson, who will be featured with his new group, the Vibrations.

Other new bookings for the same programme are P.J. Proby and Brian Mathew, who will act as guest d-j.

The only other new booking for the following week (26th) is Tony Dalli.

51

under a car was a pair of legs sticking out as this chap worked on his motor. The radio in his car was playing 'Bye, Bye Baby' and he was singing along to it. I almost felt the urge to say "That's me, mate, on that record" but I carried on walking past.

It was not unusual to get recognised in the street or on the tube after a TV appearance.

TEENBEAT TOP 20

1	I'm Into Something Good	Herman's Hermits
2	Where Did Our Love Go?	The Supremes
3	I'm Crying	The Animals
4	Rag Doll	The Four Seasons
5	I Wouldn't Trade You For The World	The Bachelors
6	When You Walk In The Room	The Searchers
7	We're Through	The Hollies
8	Have I The Right?	The Honeycombs
9	Bread And Butter	The Newbeats
10	You Really Got Me	The Kinks
11	Five By Five (EP)	Rolling Stones
12	It's Gonna Be All Right	Gerry Pacemakers
13	Seven Daffodils	The Cherokees
14	One Way Love	Cliff Bennett and Rebel Rousers
15	She's Not There	The Zombies
16	Do Wah Diddy Diddy	Manfred Mann
17	Rhythm And Greens	The Shadows
18	Seven Daffodils	The Mojos
19	Bye Bye Baby	T. Jackson/Vibrations
20	Pretty Face	The Beat Merchants

BRITAIN'S TOP 50

NATIONAL CHART COMPILED BY THE RECORD RETAILER

1 OH PRETTY WOMAN
  4 (5) Roy Orbison (London)
2 I'M INTO SOMETHING GOOD
  1 (8) Herman's Hermits (Columbia)
3 WHERE DID OUR LOVE GO
  3 (6) Supremes (Stateside)
4 RAG DOLL
  2 (7) Four Seasons (Philips)
5 THE WEDDING
  7 (9) Julie Rogers (Mercury)
6 I WOULDN'T TRADE YOU FOR THE WORLD
  9 (9) The Bachelors (Decca)
7 I WON'T FORGET YOU
  6 (17) Jim Reeves (RCA Victor)
8 TOGETHER
  11 (6) P. J. Proby (Decca)
9 WHEN YOU WALK IN THE ROOM
  16 (4) The Searchers (Pye)
10 I'M CRYING
  15 (4) Animals (Columbia)
11 EVERYBODY LOVES SOMEBODY
  12 (7) Dean Martin (Reprise)
12 AS TEARS GO BY
  9 (9) Marianne Faithfull (Decca)
13 HAVE I THE RIGHT
  8 (12) The Honeycombs (Pye)
14 WE'RE THROUGH
  20 (4) The Hollies (Parlophone)
15 BREAD AND BUTTER
  19 (5) The Newbeats (Hickory)
16 YOU REALLY GOT ME
  10 (9) The Kinks (Pye)
17 WALK AWAY
  22 (4) Matt Monro (Parlophone)
18 IS IT TRUE
  18 (5) Brenda Lee (Brunswick)
19 I LOVE YOU BECAUSE
  17 (34) Jim Reeves (RCA Victor)
20 SHE'S NOT THERE
  14 (9) The Zombies (Decca)
21 THE CRYING GAME
  13 (10) Dave Berry (Decca)
22 MAYBE I KNOW
  28 (3) Lesley Gore (Mercury)
23 HOW SOON
  31 (5) Henry Mancini (RCA Victor)
24 SUCH A NIGHT
  21 (4) Elvis Presley (RCA)
25 RHYTHM 'N' GREENS
  23 (6) Shadows (Columbia)

26 IT'S GONNA BE ALRIGHT
  26 (6) Gerry & The Pacemakers (Columbia)
27 DO WAH DIDDY DIDDY
  27 (13) Manfred Mann (HMV)
28 A HARD DAY'S NIGHT
  24 (13) Beatles (Parlophone)
29 ONE WAY LOVE
  42 (2) Cliff Bennett (Parlophone)
  TWELFTH OF NEVER
  — (1) Cliff Richard (Columbia)
  (THERE'S) ALWAYS SOMETHING THERE TO REMIND ME
  — (1) Sandie Shaw (Pye)
32 SUMMER IS OVER
  37 (2) Frank Ifield (Columbia)
33 SEVEN DAFFODILS
  25 (5) The Mojos (Decca)
  UM, UM, UM, UM, UM, UM
  — (1) Wayne Fontana (Fontana)
35 IT'S ALL OVER NOW
  32 (15) Rolling Stones (Decca)
36 HAPPINESS
  33 (12) Ken Dodd (Columbia)
37 COME TO ME
  40 (3) Julie Grant (Pye)
38 YOU NEVER CAN TELL
  29 (8) Chuck Berry (Pye)
39 IT'S FOR YOU
  35 (10) Cilla Black (Parlophone)
40 I SHOULD HAVE KNOWN BETTER
  36 (8) The Naturals (Parlophone)
  REACH OUT FOR ME
  — (1) Dionne Warwick (Pye)
42 DO I LOVE YOU
  41 (5) Ronettes (London)
43 NO ONE TO CRY TO
  38 (3) Ray Charles (HMV)
44 MECCA
  34 (3) Cheetahs (Philips)
45 REMEMBER (WALKIN' IN THE SAND)
  — (1) Shangri-Las (Red Bird)
46 BYE BYE BABY
  — (1) Tony Jackson and the Vibrations (Pye)
47 UNDER THE BOARDWALK
  45 (3) Drifters (Atlantic)
48 WHAT AM I TO YOU
  44 (6) Kenny Lynch (HMV)
49 THE LETTER
  39 (5) The Long and the Short (Decca)
50 LOVE'S MADE A FOOL OF YOU
  50 (5) Buddy Holly (Coral)

A blue dot denotes new entry.

The 1964 Points Table

BASED upon the weekly Top Thirty, compiled by the "New Musical Express"—from November, 1963, to the end of October, 1964. Thirty points awarded for top place, and so on, down to one point for 30th place.

1	BEATLES	1,812
2	BACHELORS	961
3	ROLLING STONES	909
4	JIM REEVES	831
5	CLIFF RICHARD	825
6	SEARCHERS	815
7	ROY ORBISON	734
8	DAVE CLARK FIVE	722
9	GERRY AND THE PACEMAKERS	646
10	HOLLIES	646
11	Cilla Black	634
12	Manfred Mann	618
13	Dusty Springfield	566
14	Brian Poole and the Tremeloes	557
15	Swinging Blue Jeans	534
16	Billy J. Kramer	527
17	Gene Pitney	480
18	Elvis Presley	424
19	Freddie and the Dreamers	420
20	Shadows	419
21	Merseybeats	412
22	Kathy Kirby	395
23	Animals	391
24	Peter and Gordon	380
25	Millie	345
26	Four Pennies	342
27	P.J. Proby	324
28	Fourmost	311
29	Chuck Berry	289
30	Billy Fury	272
31	Supremes	270
32	Brenda Lee	265
33	Ronettes	263
34	Dionne Warwick	252
35	Herman's Hermits	250
36	Honeycombs	241
37	Kinks	234
38	Nashville Teens	216
39	Los Indios Tabajaras	212
40	Applejacks	209
41	Four Seasons	208
42	Barron Knights	202
43	Julie Rogers	198
44	Mary Wells	197
45	Dave Berry	194
46	Louis Armstrong	187
47	Big Dee Irwin	186
48	Adam Faith	184
49	Singing Nun	177
50	Migil Five	177
51	Frank Ifield	171
52	Shirley Bassey	162
53	Doris Day	154
54	Beach Boys	143
55	Eden Kane	142
56	Dean Martin	142
57	Rick Nelson	134
58	Marianne Faithfull	133
59	Matt Monro	131
60	Lulu and the Luvers	124
61	Gigliola Cinquetti	122
62	Sandie Shaw	115
63	Mark Wynter	107

64	Zombies	106
65	Henry Mancini	102
66	Mojos	101
67	Frankie Vaughan	94
68	Crystals	86
69	Bern Elliott and the Fenmen	83
70	Peter, Paul and Mary	71
71	Trini Lopez	70
71	Kingsmen	66
73	Cliff Bennett and the Rebel Rousers	66
74	Newbeats	65
75	Heinz	63
76	Nino Tempo and April Stevens	53
77	Dora Bryan	51
78	Chris Sandford	47
79	Wayne Fontana and the Mindbenders	40
80	Everly Brothers	39
81	Jimmy Young	38
82	Lesley Gore	37
83	Carter-Lewis	36
84	Dixie Cups	35
85	John Lee Hooker	28
86	Rockin' Berries	28
87	Johnny Kidd	27
88	Tommy Tucker	25
89	Del Shannon	23
90	Ezz Reco	23
91	Tommy Roe	22
92	Kenny Ball	22
93	Ray Charles	21
93	Ken Dodd	21
95	Little Richard	21
96	Ronnie Hilton	20
97	Helmut Zacharias	19
98	Shangri-Las	18
99	Richard Anthony	17
100	Pretty Things	15
100	Top Six	14
102	Crickets	14
102	Stan Getz-Joao Gilberto	11
102	Joy Strings	11
102	Naturals	11
106	Harry H. Corbett and Wilfrid Brambell	9
106	Harry Secombe	9
108	Tony Jackson	7
108	Tony Meehan (3 with Jet Harris)	7
110	Fats Domino	6
110	Yardbirds	6
112	Karl Denver	5
112	Terry Stafford	5
114	Gamblers	4
115	Cherokees	4
115	Julie Grant	3
117	Val Doonican	2
117	Downliners Sect	2
119	Ella Fitzgerald	1
119	Major Lance	1
119	Martha and the Vandellas	1
119	Poets	1

Last week's placings in brackets

1	(2)	OH, PRETTY WOMAN	Roy Orbison
2	(1)	I'M INTO SOMETHING GOOD	Herman's Hermits
3	(3)	WHERE DID OUR LOVE GO	Supremes
4	(4)	RAG DOLL	Four Seasons
5	(6)	THE WEDDING	Julie Rogers
6	(10)	I'M CRYING	Animals
7	(5)	I WOULDN'T TRADE YOU FOR THE WORLD	Bachelors
8	(15)	WE'RE THROUGH	Hollies
9	(14)	WHEN YOU WALK IN THE ROOM	Searchers
10	(8)	TOGETHER	P. J. Proby
11	(13)	EVERYBODY LOVES SOMEBODY	Dean Martin
12	(—)	ALWAYS SOMETHING THERE TO REMIND ME	Sandie Shaw
13	(—)	TWELFTH OF NEVER	Cliff Richard
14	(21)	WALK AWAY	Matt Monro
15	(7)	I WON'T FORGET YOU	Jim Reeves
16	(18)	HOW SOON	Henry Mancini
17	(9)	YOU REALLY GOT ME	Kinks
18	(17)	BREAD AND BUTTER	Newbeats
19	(16)	AS TEARS GO BY	Marianne Faithfull
20	(19)	IS IT TRUE	Brenda Lee
21	(28)	ONE WAY LOVE	Cliff Bennett and the Rebel Rousers
22	(26)	MAYBE I KNOW	Lesley Gore
23	(16)	THE CRYING GAME	Dave Berry
24	(12)	HAVE I THE RIGHT	Honeycombs
25	(—)	BYE BYE BABY	Tony Jackson
26	(—)	REACH OUT FOR ME	Dionne Warwick
27	(—)	UM, UM, UM, UM, UM, UM	Wayne Fontana and the Mindbenders
28	(—)	QUESTIONS I CAN'T ANSWER	Heinz
29	(20)	SHE'S NOT THERE	Zombies
30	(30)	SUMMER IS OVER	Frank Ifield

By arrangement with "New Musical Express"

* JUNE's DATE with...

TONY JACKSON
and The VIBRATIONS

WHEN I heard Tony Jackson was leaving The Searchers, I was very sad! But now that I have heard Tony's first non-Searcher record, I think it was a good thing.

The record, as you will know, is called *Bye Bye Baby*.

On this disc, the earthy sound of *Sugar and Spice* is put over twice as strongly by Tony singing over his own voice, making it sound like two Tony Jacksons. (Not bad for the price of one, eh ?)

Singing and playing with Tony are three very capable young musicians who go under the name of The Vibrations.

When Tony left The Searchers, his first problem was to find a backing group. Word soon got round, and applications poured in by the dozen without Tony even having advertised.

A special report on the ex-Searcher and his great new group by MOIRA

One of the boys who wrote to Tony for an audition was Ian Buisel, a twenty-year-old lead guitarist. Ian had a friend, Martin, who played the organ and piano, and persuaded him to go along to the audition with him at The Roaring Twenties Club in London.

" The auditions were supposed to start at mid-day," said Martin. " But we waited for ages outside the place, and no one came to let us in ! We were just about to go away at one o'clock when the door opened ! "

Phew ! That was a near thing ! We nearly didn't have any Vibrations !

" There were about a hundred people to audition," said Tony, " but when the other organists heard Martin, they just walked out—he was so good ! "

The third member of the group —seventeen-year-old Paul Francis—is the drummer.

But young though he is, Paul has had a lot of experience. He has played in many local groups, as well as Bobby Cristo and The Rebels, and Rolf Harris's backing group.

Paul will tell you that he had seen Martin and Ian around but had never spoken to them before the day of the audition. He lives in Barking and, like Barking's other famous sons, Brian Poole and The Tremeloes, he is a very good musician !

I spoke to the boys in Tony Jackson's Kensington flat, where I was given a steaming hot cup of coffee and asked anxiously what I thought of *Bye Bye Baby*.

Pleasantly modest, that's Tony.

Born in Liverpool on 16th July, 1940, Tony had various jobs, including apprentice electrician, before joining The Searchers at the age of twenty. That was when he made his first public appearance—in Liverpool.

Tony's first home-town solo appearance was in early October this year.

Now, some personal facts. He is 5 ft. 9 in. tall and has dark brown hair and sad grey eyes. He values genuine friends and dislikes people who laugh at others' misfortunes. (Good for him !)

In his soft Liverpool voice, he told me of the split with The Searchers.

" I couldn't agree with the others about songs ! " he admitted honestly. " I like rhythm and blues type music—but the others weren't keen. Now that I've left The Searchers, I can play what I like ! "

I think Tony is right to like rhythm and blues—he has that sort of voice and will go far with that type of singing.

Tony and the boys told me the story behind their first disc.

" I heard the original recording of *Bye Bye Baby* on an LP I had," Tony explained. " I was wandering round singing it to myself, and didn't realise what it was. So I thought if I can remember it—other people will, too !

" We started to rehearse here, (at his flat) but the neighbours rang the housing agents, complaining. We were warned that if we didn't stop the racket, they would throw me out ! "

I suppose everyone can't be expected to like hearing Tony Jackson and The Vibrations rehearsing. But if I were living next-door to them, I wouldn't mind a bit, would you ?

Below : l. to r. : Ian Buisel (guitar), Martin Raymond (organist), Tony Jackson and Paul Francis (drummer).

NEXT WEEK : The day THE ZOMBIES invaded the JUNE office.

I have never really understood the fascination people have about people on TV, but it does help to promote records and for that we were most grateful. What I was not really prepared for were the screaming girls who would try to grab your hair, or clothing.

Above: Paul on tour, signing autographs

Malcolm our road manager was a big guy so he came in useful to keep people at bay. Because of his size the girls could not push past him very easily.

Signing autographs was never a problem. We always obliged. Our main concern was on stage. There would hardly ever be all four members on stage at once due to members being pulled off by the girls in the audience. They would even get up behind the drums and pull me off. It was funny, but it took time out of our set and we really just wanted to play which was impossible.

About this time the Rebels had changed their name to Bobby Rio and the Revelles and had also signed to Pye Records. I was asked to play

53

on 'Don't Break My Heart And Run Away' the B-side of their single which was to be recorded in Joe Meek's studio at 304 Holloway Road. The studio was a flat above a shop. The sessions went fine and Joe was easy to get on with that day. An excellent film came out in 2009 about Joe Meek called Telstar. Clem Cattini is featured in the film with the Tornados and he had a cameo part as a taxi driver.

All too quickly it was time to start the tour. It was to be for 29 dates with two shows an evening from 19th September until 18th October with no days off. We were with The Hollies and Freddie and

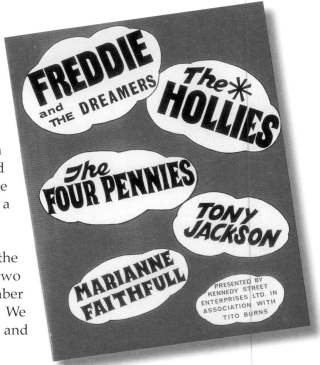

The Dreamers, Marianne Faithfull, The Four Pennies, and The Toggery Five a new band from Manchester. The Compare was Don Dwight.

The Toggery Five opened the show followed by Don Dwight, then us and The Four Pennies closed the first half. After an interval The Toggery Five came on again, then Marianne Faithfull, The Hollies and Freddy and The Dreamers closed the show. Why they closed I will never know. To my mind The Hollies should have closed the show. The Hollies were, and still are, a fantastic group. Their musicianship was great. Vocal-wise there was nobody to touch them, and to top it all there was Bobby Elliott on drums. Bob is a fantastic player and was always a pleasure to watch from the wings. Great press rolls and catching the cymbal from underneath with the stick. Bob has a sound of his own and a style that when you hear it you know it is Bobby Elliott. He is another good friend that I have known a long while now. I first met Bobby in the early sixties outside a music shop in Shaftesbury Avenue, London, when he was working with Shane Fenton and the Fentones.

Freddie and The Dreamers were great fun in the dressing room and we always had a good laugh with them. To give Freddie and The Dreamers their due, they put on a good show which was mainly comedy and it did go down well. But The Hollies are a hard act to follow. Bernie Dwyer, the Dreamer's drummer also played a Trixon kit and said I could use his kit for the tour. Bobby also said I could use his Ludwig kit. I went for the Trixon. I must have been mad as the Ludwig

Above: Bobby Elliott and Paul

was a far superior kit, but I guess I thought I would stick with the one I knew. Poor Bernie never tuned it much so it was never the best sounding kit but I tweaked it up a bit and felt comfortable with it.

All the acts travelled on a coach which made it more fun on the road. This time we stayed at Hotels and only very rarely did we have to share a room. We were also able to get room service at night which was always handy after a show. The artists would often play practical jokes on one another. Alan Clarke the lead singer with The Hollies was sitting behind me one day and I heard him saying he did not feel very well. He stood up and lent over my seat. "I don't feel too good" he said "I think I'm going to be sick" and made the sound of being sick then threw handfuls of torn up paper over me. For a split second I thought he had been sick over me. We all laughed, it was a good trick.

I got my own back later by getting under the stage where in those days the mic stands came up from under the stage. I moved it very slowly so that Alan had to get lower and lower, then it came back up again. It must have looked funny from the front. Then it was someone else's turn for their stand to move. Poor Tony Hicks and Graham Nash had to go along with it. No one got angry as it was just a bit of fun.

The Toggery Five and The Four Pennies did good sets. Fritz Fryer the guitarist with the Four Pennies was always good fun. Marianne Faithfull sang with a guitarist backing her. She had a soft voice, not very strong, but she looked stunning, really pretty.

56

The Toggery Five took their name from a clothes shop of the same name in Manchester. The owner, Michael Cohen, managed them and The Hollies. The shop did great clothes so we always looked forward to calling in there.

On our gigs before the tour you could get about and nip over the pub for a drink but with this package tour there were great packs of girls waiting outside the stage door so it had to be worked out how we could get to the pub without being seen. That never happened, but sometimes we could get a start on them and leg it as fast as we could only to find the same problem getting back. Normally our road manager would go on ahead and get the stage door open.

We did make it to one pub but the girls came in after us and the landlord said we would have to go in the restaurant in the back. This was a good idea as we could get something to eat. We sat down and were eating our soup when the window across the restaurant flew open right where a couple were eating and girls started to climb in over their table. We started throwing bread rolls at them for a laugh. The couple were not amused!

We played for about half an hour on the show so once we had finished we would have time to kill waiting for the show to end. After the show many of the acts would meet up in the Hotel bar. It was a good way of relaxing. The Vibrations would sometimes find shoes left outside guests' rooms waiting to be cleaned. These would be filled with shaving foam. On one occasion a Hotel Inspector was staying at the Hotel unknown to us. He was going to give the Hotel back one of the stars that it had lost. His shoes were given the Vibration treatment and as we checked out in the morning the poor Hotel owner was being informed by the Inspector what had happened. I somehow doubt he got that star back!

It was good fun having everyone on the bus. Marianne was very quiet but enjoyed a good laugh. Her act was a good contrast to the rest of the show which was more up tempo. Her hit 'As Tears Go By' always went down well.

I have never enjoyed alcohol that much as I have a sweet tooth and it was always too bitter for me. I enjoy the odd glass of wine or lager. Once we were in a pub with The Hollies before a show and they gave me a glass of cider to try. Being sweet it went down very well and they bought me several more. But unknown to me it was cider straight from the wood; very strong. When we got outside and we made our way to the theatre it hit me.

When the Vibrations went on I went on first and was announced, then one by one the others would follow with Tony being last. I would start playing as soon as I sat down. The only problem this time was I fell over the drum kit. The floor tom rolled

VIBRATING INTO FIRST RATING

The boy who broke away is going to make the big break through.

INTERVIEWED FOR YOU—THE BOY WHO WANTED TO MAKE IT ON HIS OWN.

HE used to be a Searcher, but things weren't quite right. He found that the Searchers weren't playing his kind of music any more.

Tony Jackson has always preferred the wilder, earthier sound. This is the main reason why he left the group.

But Tony wasn't lost without his three friends. He set to work straight away to get himself a group, with the sound that he wants, and have a new nose, too.

Tony said, "I've never liked my nose (the old one that is) it used to make me hide away in corners. It was horrible!"

Life is very exciting for Tony at the moment. He's busy on tour with Freddie and the Hollies, and pushing the group's first disc, "Bye Bye Baby"—a Mary Wells number.

His group, the Vibrations, are all young lads, and Tony realises that as he's been through the ropes before, it's up to him to keep an eye on them all the time.

Tony's got Ian Buisell, 20, on lead and rhythm guitar; Paul Francis, 17, on drums; and Martin Raymond, 18, on organ. The organ is a very important feature of this group's sound. In fact, Tony's raving mad about the organ.

"What with me being from Liverpool," said Tony, "and the boys being from London, we have quite a lot of laughs about one another's accents. They just won't understand that mine's the right accent!"

But whatever differences all the boys have in background, they have very quickly knitted themselves together to be one of the best new groups in the country! Tony's made sure of that. You should see the way he fusses round his group at photo sessions. He straightens their ties and collars, and generally makes sure that 'his' boys are keeping up to the standards he's set for them. And judging by Tony's standards they must be aiming quite high!

BOYFRIEND'S STAR SPREAD

STARS IN THEIR OWN RIGHT!

VIBRATING VIBRATING VIBRATING

FOR SALE...
CLEANING RAG
ENQUIRE WITHIN.

down towards the lights at the front of the stage.   I went over, panic hit me.   I got up, straightened the kit and a couple of stage hands helped retrieve my floor tom.

While this was going on The Hollies were in fits of laughter in the wings.   I managed to do the set but I was ill later.   That never happened again; I stuck to orange juice.

One other nasty experience I had was when the acts had been invited to a big party after the show.   Taxis were laid on to take us to the venue.   There was a very large crowd of screaming girls outside trying to grab artists as they got in the taxis.   We were one of the last groups to leave.   We made a run for the taxi.   I was last to get in.

I was grabbed from behind by this rather large girl.   She got hold of my tie which was leather and pulled.   The knot went really tight and I had trouble trying to breathe. Then I heard something tearing.   Malcolm our roadie had waded in to get her off.   He was a big guy but even he had problems getting her off.   When he did break her grip on me I fell into the taxi and we drove off.

The others said "Blimey Paul, you're bleeding and your shirt collar's hanging off!"   She had ripped it nearly off and the blood was from a wound on my neck caused by her finger nails.   Someone else had been pulling my hair.   I looked like Ken Dodd!

When we arrived at the party I said I could not go in looking like that.   Our suit cases were still at the theatre.   The driver said he could take me back so I could change and then bring me to the party.   Great idea I thought.   So the others filed into the house where the party was and I went back in the taxi.   The driver said "Don't worry there won't be anyone around by the time we get back."

We arrived back at the theatre and the driver parked outside and said he would walk round to the stage door to make sure it was all clear and for me to wait in the taxi.   He disappeared round the corner.   Everything was going to plan and I relaxed.   Then to my horror screaming girls came from the other corner of the theatre.   They headed straight for the taxi.   I quickly locked the doors.   In no time the taxi was surrounded. They were like ants all over it and trying to get in.   Then they started rocking the taxi from side to side.   At this point I was getting really worried.   I could not talk to them like that, they were hysterical.   Hearing all the noise the taxi driver plus members of the theatre staff arrived and started to get them off and we drove round to the stage door. I changed very quickly I might add.   Then it was in the taxi and back to the party.   For the Beatles and Stones it must have been a nightmare.   They had it all the time.   No wonder the Beatles stopped doing live shows.   They could never hear themselves for all the screaming.

Martin and I had our suits stolen at the Manchester Odeon on 8th October but we did not realise this until we arrived in Sheffield the next day. It took 3 days to get replacement suits. The last night of the tour was hilarious. Everyone was trying to sabotage the other acts. When Marianne was halfway through a slow number Freddy Garrity walked slowly across the stage dressed in a night shirt carrying a lit candle. He looked like Wee Willy Winkie! He never said a word. The place erupted with laughter. It was brilliant.

One trick that caught us out was a piece of rope tied to the drum stool. You could never see it in the dark as you walked on to take your place. The lights would go up, we would start playing and, wallop, over I would go, or some other poor soul. Firing pea shooters from the orchestra pit was fun; trying to pick off individual members of the band playing. Smoke bombs would land on stage and stink bombs. They were terrible. Heaven knows what the audience must have thought; probably that it was part of the show!

We were playing our set when Graham Nash walked on stage, sat down on an amplifier and started reading a newspaper. Then Alan Clarke came on, walked up to Graham and lit his paper with a cigarette lighter. It was done so sneakily that Graham had not seen him do it. He thought he was just joining him. The paper went up in flames. Graham put it out and walked off stage.

Footballs were often kicked onto the stage and usually got booted back or into the audience. I don't know how we got away with it. You would never be able to do it nowadays.

One night I walked upstairs and found a small office and went in. There was a record player with an LP of marching band music already on the turntable. I switched it on. The Four Pennies were on stage at the time singing their big hit, a ballad, 'Juliet'. All of a sudden the marching music came blasting out all over the theatre. It was brilliant. The poor band had to stop. I turned it off and got out of there quickly. They never did find out who did it.

Sadly the tour had come to an end. It had been a great experience and good fun and we had good audiences. It was a strong bill and a fantastic bunch of people to work with. What more could I ask for?

Over the next few months we had more TV and radio shows to do plus working round the clubs and ballrooms. At some point we played at The Cavern Club in Liverpool which was great fun.

TONY JACKSON and the VIBRATIONS—a 'by request' portrait

We did Top of the Pops on 22nd October which was a fun show to do. Wayne Fontana and The Mindbenders and Manfred Mann were also on. Both Top of the Pops and Ready, Steady, Go! had studio audiences which created a good atmosphere. Bands really thought they had made it if they appeared on these TV shows. The warm-up dancer on Ready, Steady, Go! was Paul Raven who went on to become Gary Glitter. We also had to start thinking about doing a follow up single to Bye, Bye Baby.

On one occasion The Small Faces were booked to do the Ready Steady Go TV show but Steve Marriott was reported to be suffering from exhaustion and was recovering at home. I went to visit him at his parents' flat and we went out for a walk along the river bank. He said he was fine, just a little tired. It was then that he offered me a puff on his cigarette which had marijuana in it. I was not too keen, but he assured me it was fine. So I gave it a go. We laughed a lot on the way back to his flat and I made my way back to Barking. That was the first time I had ever taken it and it was a strange feeling, but not unpleasant. I told Denis about it when I got home.

A few weeks later the band were given a little by someone so we thought we would smoke it. The trouble was that it was before we went on stage. Ian and I had a real problem concentrating on what we were doing. I can remember stopping a song and thinking it had ended when in fact it had only just started! Poor Tony was trying to give us signs when to stop. It was hilarious, but not something to be proud of.

We thought we'd bring you all the drama of Emergency Ward 10, but we couldn't quite make it, so FAB presents its own soap opera... Emergency Ward 8½!

Right: FAB Magazine 21st November 1964. Tony Jackson and the Vibrations with Gerry Marsden and Sandie Shaw

7 Susie and Dr. Killjoy try to reach a diagnosis. The patient's blood pressure has risen sharply since his admittance to EW8½. He's nearly at the top of the chart.

8 "It's gonna be all right," wails the Doc. But Sister Susie isn't so sure. But the jealous Doc. and pretty nurse agree on one thing ... Rock's ailment is a major one. He's in love.

5 Psychiatrists are called in to talk to Rock; to see if the shock has unbalanced him. They believe they can sort out his problem.

6 Ah, well—better luck next time! Would anyone like to volunteer to sort out three mixed-up psychiatrists?

We used to carry a soda siphon in the van which gave us endless hours of fun squirting at people. Tony would always be in the back saying "No. Don't do it." Then he would shout "Go on. Squirt him now." When we did Tony would laugh so much he would have to use his inhaler as he suffered quite badly with asthma.

We were booked to do our next recording at Pye Studios in December 1964. We tried various numbers and the two we chose were 'You Beat Me To The Punch' for the A-side and 'This Little Girl Of Mine' as the B-side. This Little Girl was a Ray Charles song which Tony liked. A fast track compared to the A-side which was a mid tempo track and Ian sang the high harmony. I must say it did sound a little like The Searchers with acoustic guitars and Ian's harmony.

'You Beat Me to The Punch' had a lot of air plays and again we did various TV and Radio shows to promote it including Ready Steady Go on 11th December 1964. A rare clip of this performance appeared on Youtube in 2010 which was great to see. Gerry and The Pacemakers, Georgie Fame and The Blue Flames and Kenny Lynch were also on this show. During my time with The Vibrations we were often on Ready Steady Go and Thank Your Lucky Stars to promote various singles.

On 9th January 1965 when we were on Thank Your Lucky Stars The Kinks were also on that show. We liked their recording of 'You Really Got Me'. Dave Clark was also on the show and he came to say hello. A nice chap. He was also a very good business man. The Dave Clark Five were massive in America.

Above: Paul & Ian on Ready Steady Go! "You Beat Me to The Punch"

64

The following day on 10th January we played at the ABC Commodore, Hammersmith. Top of the bill were The Rolling Stones. The other acts were Zoot Money and The Big Roll Band, Marianne Faithfull, Julie Grant, The Original Checkmates, Tony Marsh and The Quiet Five.

Unfortunately 'You Beat Me to The Punch' failed to chart, so it was back to the drawing board for our next single. 'Love Potion No. 9' which had already been done by The Searchers with Tony singing was suggested. We were not keen on this idea, but various people said it had not been a single in the UK, so we went ahead with it.

JACKSON, SEARCHERS BURY THE HATCHET

NEW single from ex-Searcher Tony Jackson, out tomorrow (Friday) is "Love Potion Number 9" the song with which the Searchers reached the number two position recently in the American chart.

And ironically, that Searchers' smash-hit featured Tony as lead singer. It was recorded before he left the group to solo. Tito Burns, agent for both the Searchers

and Jackson and the Vibrations, said this week that the famous feud between Tony and his old group was now over. "They shook hands in this office", said Burns. "It was silly for them to continue this battle."

Jackson features his new record on ITV's "Eamonn Andrews Show" this Sunday; Granada TV's "Scene At 6.30" (February 8); ITV's "Ready, Steady, Go!" (12) and "Lucky Stars" (20).

TONY JACKSON AND THE VIBRATIONS

LOVE Potion No. 9 (Pye). I have always thought this a splendid song with words like "When I kissed a cop down on 34th and Vine" and I must say I quite like Tony's version of this even though I do remember the original by The Clovers.

Nice organ and drum combination at the beginning.

AVAILABLE TOMORROW.

Two other tips for the Top Ten: ex-Searchers Tony Jackson and The Vibrations with *Love Potion No. 9* (Pye), which is first-rate fun about a gipsy curing a boy who's a flop with the girls. And Gene Pitney's *I Must Be Seeing Things* (Stateside), a tear-laden piece about losing a girl.

'Love Potion No. 9' was produced by Larry Page and came out in February 1965. It charted at number 37 in the UK and number 12 in Sweden on 27th March.

We did a great version of 'Fortune Teller' for the B- side which we had really wanted as the A-side. I loved Ian's guitar on that number. We had tried to get the distortion that the Kinks had on the guitar of 'You Really Got Me' and it worked.

BRITISH HIT 100

THEY CAME ROLLING HOME!

Andrew Oldham and Brian Harvey listen to tapes of the Stones new sessions.

Pos	LW	Artist	Title
1	24	ROLLING STONES	The Last Time
2	1	TOM JONES	It's Not Unusual
3	3	SEEKERS	I'll Never Find Another You
4		WAYNE FONTANA/MINDBENDERS	Game Of Love
5	4	HERMAN'S HERMITS	Silhouettes
6	11	SANDIE SHAW	I'll Stop At Nothing/You Can't Blame Him
7	12	MARIANNE FAITHFULL	Come Stay With Me
8	9	VAL DOONICAN	The Special Years
9		HOLLIES	Yes I Will
10	8	ANIMALS	Don't Let Me Be Misunderstood
11		IVY LEAGUE	Funny How Love Can Be
12	7	GENE PITNEY	I Must Be Seeing Things
13	5	KINKS	Tired Of Waiting For You
14	15	ROY ORBISON	Goodnight
15	10	P. J. PROBY	I Apologise
16	18	SHADOWS	Mary Ann
17	17	DEL SHANNON	Keep Searchin'
18	55	SEARCHERS	Goodbye My Love
19		JIM REEVES	It Hurts So Much
20	27	RONNIE HILTON	Windmill In Old Amsterdam
21	20	PRETTY THINGS	Honey I Need
22	13	RIGHTEOUS BROTHERS	You've Lost That Lovin' Feeling
23	22	TWINKLE	Golden Lights
24	—	GEORGIE FAME	In The Meantime
25	19	MANFRED MANN	Come Tomorrow
26	21	SOUNDS ORCHESTRAL	Cast Your Fate To The Winds
27	28	ADAM FAITH	Stop Feelin' Sorry For Yourself
28	40	THE WHO	I Can't Explain
29	35	GOLDIE AND THE GINGERBREADS	Can't You Hear My Heartbeat
30	25	MOODY BLUES	Go Now
31	33	UNIT FOUR PLUS TWO	Concrete And Clay
32	31	PET CLARKE	I Know A Place
33	30	DOBIE GRAY	The In Crowd
34	28	KATHY KIRBY	I Belong
35	23	SHANGRI-LAS	Leader of the Pack
36	32	THEM	Baby Please Don't Go
37	38	TONY JACKSON	Love Potion No. 9
38	33	ZOMBIES	Tell Her No
39		NASHVILLE TEENS	Find My Way Back Home
40	36	DUSTY SPRINGFIELD	Your Hurtin' Kind Of Love
41	58	WAIKIKIS	Hawaiian Tattoo
42	34	SUE THOMSON	Paper Tiger
43	—	ELVIS PRESLEY	Do The Clam
44	43	HEINZ	Diggin' My Potatoes
45	50	GEORGIE FAME	Yeh Yeh
46		SPENCER DAVIS GROUP	
47	45	SHIRLEY ELLIS	Every Little Bit Hurts
48	44	ROCKIN' BERRIES	The Name Game
49	41	TWINKLE	What In The World's Come Over You
50		VAL DOONICAN	Walk Tall
51	31	BILLY FURY	I'm Lost Without You
52	62	BILLY J. KRAMER	It's Gotta Last For Ever
53	42	BRIAN POOLE	Three Bells
54	32	CILLA BLACK	You've Lost That Lovin' Feeling
55	53	LARRY CUNNINGHAM	Tribute to Jim Reeves
56	56	CHUCK BERRY	Promised Land
57		CLIFF RICHARD	The Minute You've Gone
58		CLIFF RICHARD	I'll Take You Home
59	74	PETULA CLARK	Down Town
60	52	BO DIDDLEY	Hey Good Lookin'
61	60	TENNASEANS	You Are My Love
62	13	AD LIBS	Boy From New York City
63	83	P J PROBY	Somewhere
64	—	SUPREMES	Come See About Me
65	65	BETTY EVERETT	Getting Mighty Crowded
67	67	T. BONES	Give Him One More Chance
68	68	RON AND MEL	Shabby Little Hut
		DAVE DEE DOZIE BEAKY MICH TICH	No Time
69		BACHELORS	No Arms Could Ever Hold You
70		YARDBIRDS	For Your Love
71		POETS	That's The Way
72		DAVE CLARK FIVE	Reelin' and Rockin'
73		CRAIG DOUGLAS	Across The Street
74		FRANKIE VAUGHAN	Someone Must Have Hurt You A Lot
75	57	JEWEL AKENS	Birds and the Bees
76		JOE BROWN	Teardrops In The Rain
77	29	GERRY AND THE PACEMAKERS	Ferry 'Cross The Mersey
78		KEELY SMITH	You're Breaking My Heart
79		PEGGY LEE	Pass Me By
80	77	JIM REEVES	There's A Heartache Following Me
81	80	DORIA TROY	Watcha Gonna Do About It
82	82	RONNIE CARROLL	Dear Heart
83	—	BEAU BRUMMELL	I Know, Know Know
84	81	BERT WEEDON	12 String Guitar
85	61	JULIE ANDREWS	Spoonful Of Sugar
86	—	NAT KING COLE	L-O-V-E
87	83	ROGER MILLER	King Of The Road
88	—	FOUR SEASONS	Bye Bye Baby
89		JOHNNY RIVERS	Midnight Special
90		JIMMY RADCLIFFE	Long After The Night
91	97	RONETTES	Born To Be Together
92	—	EVERLY BROTHERS	You're My Girl
93		FOUR PENNIES	Way Of Love
94		DAVE CLARK 5	Everybody Knows
95	49	SANDIE SHAW	Girl Don't Come
96	47	BEACH BOYS	Dance, Dance, Dance
97	55	THE BEATLES	I Feel Fine
98		BABBITY BLUE	Don't Make Me
99		MATT MONRO	Without You
100	87	JAMES BROWN	Night Train

27 mars 1965			
1	(1)	ROCK AND ROLL MUSIC	The Beatles
2	(2)	THE LAST TIME	The Rolling Stones
3	(4)	LITTLE EGYPT	Downliners Sect
4	(2)	I SHOULD BE GLAD	Tages
5	(5)	TIRED OF WAITING FOR YOU	The Kinks
6	(6)	DON'T LET ME BE MISUNDERSTOOD	The Animals
7	(6)	I GO TO PIECES	Peter & Gordon
8	(8)	YES I WILL	The Hollies
8	(—)	A TRIBUTE TO BUDDY HOLLY	The Hep Stars
10	(—)	SHE'S NOT THERE	Ola & The Janglers
11	(10)	I'LL NEVER FIND ANOTHER YOU	The Seekers
12	(—)	LOVE POTION NO. 9	Tony Jackson & The Vibrations
13	(9)	DIS-MOI POURQUOI	Bob Asklöf
13	(15)	LONG TALL SHORTY	The Deejays
15	(14)	NEW ORLEANS	The Namelosers

We promoted this single on The Eamonn Andrews Show on 7th February 1965. Other artists on the show were Barbara Cartland, Roger Moore, Ted Ray and Sandie Shaw. We also did Thank Your Lucky Stars on 20th February with The Shadows, The Pretty Things and Sandie Shaw. Brian Matthew was one of the host presenters on Thank Your Lucky Stars which was pre-recorded. Brian also did a good radio show called Saturday Club which had live bands. We did a session for him in 1965. Many years later on Brian continued to promote the sixties bands with The Sounds of The Sixties radio programme.

It was agreed that Tony should get a bass player in the band and that would leave him free to move about the stage more. Denis, my friend and Rebels bass player joined, which was great. He was a good bass player. I was still lodging with his family in Barking so it worked out really

Above:
The Eamonn
Andrews Show
7th February
1965

67

well for both of us.   I thought Tony's style of playing was good, he would keep it simple and it worked.   The bass on 'Sweets for My Sweet' is a good example.   Denis had a different style and was a more advanced player and we worked well together, so it did not take long to get the band tight.   Normally it takes time to get a new rhythm section working together well but the fact that we had played together before worked in our favour.   Tony enjoyed not having to worry about playing and singing at the same time.   The Vibrations would play a couple of numbers before Tony came on stage, which unfortunately left Tony on his own so he was able to have a drink to give him a bit of confidence.

In the middle of March Tony was involved in a fight in a bar when a guy went for him with a broken bottle.   It cut the underside of Tony's arm very badly and he had stitches from his wrist nearly up to his elbow.

One night on stage during the start of the next tour he misjudged where the orchestra pit was as it was covered over and Tony went straight in.   Eventually a bloody hand appeared and he hauled himself back on stage.   He had opened the stitches and the arm was bleeding.   We carried on and finished the show.

Another time at a venue up north some chap called out something to Tony referring to the fact that he was wearing make up.   The next thing we knew Tony jumped off the stage and went for this chap whacking him with the mic stand.   The man ran off.   Tony calmly got back on stage and said "Right.   Does anyone else want to call me anything?" We finished the show thinking that was the end of it only to have a brick come smashing through our dressing room window!   We managed to leave without any more trouble.

DUSTY, ZOMBIES, VEE, SEARCHERS TOUR SET

A SCHEDULE of dates has been fixed for the Dusty Springfield-Searchers-Zombies-Tony Jackson tour. Promoter Tito Burns has added Bobby Vee to the package as special guest star. He has also fixed TV and radio appearances for Vee in connection with the singer's new Liberty single "Cross My Heart" (his own composition) which is almost certainly being issued here on March 19.

As revealed in the NME a fortnight ago, the tour opens at Stockton Odeon on March 25. Other venues set for next month are Newcastle City Hall (26th), Doncaster Gaumont (27th), and Liverpool Empire (28th).

In April the package plays Gaumont theatres at Worcester (1st) and Bradford (3rd), and Odeons at Colchester (7th), Salisbury (8th) and Taunton (9th).

Remainder of the April dates are Birmingham Town Hall (2nd), Bristol Colston (4th) and Cardiff Sophia Gardens (10th).

We now had a tour lined up starting on 25th March in Stockton with 11 dates ending on 10th April at Cardiff Sophia Gardens. The line up this time was The Searchers, Dusty Springfield, The Zombies, and Heinz and the Wild Boys who had gone solo from The Tornados. Bobby Vee from the States was also on and George Meaton was the compere. He pulled great faces. The Echoes were backing Dusty and also played a set themselves.

The running order was The Echoes, George Meaton then us, followed by Bobby Vee with Dusty closing the first half. The Echoes opened the second half followed by George, The Zombies, Heinz and the Wild Boys, with The Searchers closing the show.

The strain was starting to tell with Tony and I think being on with The Searchers he felt he had more to prove. We would go on and do a good set but Tony was drinking more which could be a problem at times. Tony never really wanted to be up front as the vocalist. He was more at ease playing bass as part of the band.

The Zombies were a good band and The Echoes did a good job backing Dusty who had a fabulous voice. She was quite a shy person off stage, but once you got talking to her and shared a joke she was fine. Dusty died in 1999 aged 59. There was no mistaking her voice, she was unique. She made some great records.

The tour was not quite the same as the last tour. The Searchers were never going to be over

friendly because of the split with Tony. They kept themselves to themselves most of the time. However, Tony and Mike Pender got on well even after the split. I did not take to Chris Curtis as a person but to give him his due he was a good showman. He would stand up whilst playing the drums and he would sing and wave his sticks around in the air. Frank and John were fine. Bobby Vee was very quiet on the coach, you never knew he was there. He had quite a few hits. 'The Night Has a Thousand Eyes' was very popular.

The Vibrations were on their own this time with practical jokes. Bobby Vee would be standing in the wings waiting to go on and the compere would say "Ladies and Gentlemen, Bobby Vee." Just as he went to walk on we held him back. The compere would repeat it. After about the third time we would let him go. Another good wheeze was on Heinz. He would come off stage and while the band was still playing he would change into a different outfit in the wings. We would tie knots in his trousers. He would be rushing to get dressed only to find the knotted trousers. He took the joke well. We never bothered with The Searchers. Somehow I don't think they would have appreciated it. The Zombies were OK, certain members could take a joke. We would make Dusty laugh by doing something in the wings, but we never sabotaged her act.

The theatres had a speaker in each dressing room where you could hear the acts on stage. Acts would also be told how long before they were due on stage. We had to turn it off when Heinz was on. He was the vocal equivalent to Les Dawson's piano playing when he hit all the bum notes, but he was a nice enough chap.

I remember a show when he came off stage while the band played on. He would go out the stage door into a waiting taxi, drive to the front of the theatre then come running down the aisle and up onto the stage again and finish the song. Only this time for some reason the band had stopped playing and the theatre had brought down the safety curtain for the interval. The lady was at the front of the stage selling ice creams as Heinz came roaring down the aisle only to be confronted with no band and the house lights full on. It was so funny. Backstage the air was blue in his dressing room as he had a go at his band for stopping, saying they had made him look a right fool.

We did another venue with him where the audience also sat behind the stage. Some chap sitting in the front threw an opened can of baked beans at Heinz. It missed him only to go all over one of the men sitting behind the band. A fight nearly broke out as abuse was shouted out. Poor Heinz and the band played on. It was not unusual to have toys thrown on stage by fans. I remember a Swiss roll once but luckily it did not hit anyone. Barry Tomlinson the guitarist with The Chessmen later went on to work with Heinz in his band.

For five weeks after the tour we gigged up and down the country with only the occasional day off. Tony fell ill with tonsillitis for 5 days towards the end of April and we had to cancel some bookings. Mike Cummings was now the roadie. We nicknamed him Swenowa because of the way he mumbled when he spoke.

During all the touring there were only really casual flings with girls who had been to a show. One night two attractive girls arrived backstage to say hello. They were dancers. Martin hit it off with Lesley and I got on well with Marilyn. She lived in

Nottingham which made it difficult to sustain a relationship. I did visit her at her parents' house a few times and she also came down to London and Kent. I liked her a lot but because of her dancing career and my music and living so far apart the relationship gradually ended.

From 17th May until the 27th we visited Norway for some gigs and a TV show. The gigs were packed mainly with women, and the TV was fun. It was while doing that show one of the members of a Swedish band also playing informed us that we had three records in the Swedish top 30! It was something we knew nothing about. He said people would love to see us in Sweden. We telephoned Tito Burns to see if we could go over there as we were very close being in Norway. He said he would fix something up later on, but that never happened. We had many requests from fans to go there. That was a big mistake by the management.

We had recorded a new single in April which was produced at Pye by Alan A. Freeman. The A-side was a ballad called 'Stage Door' by Goffin and King, with 'That's What I Want' on the B-side. This record was released in July 1965. Tony sang it really well but it did not chart.

On the 12th July 1965 we were on the Gadzooks! It's All Happening TV show along with Tom Jones and Vikki Carr. We also did Thank Your Lucky Stars on 24th July with The Yardbirds including Jeff Beck, Mike Berry, The Honeycombs, Vikki Carr and Jackie Trent.

On our return from Norway the bookings were quite thin on the ground so it was decided we would go to Germany from 29th July until 7th August. We had a booking at the Star-Club

Above: Norway, May 1965. Tony, Paul, Martin, Denis, Ian

"THE BEAT SCENE IS DYING" SAYS EX SEARCHER TONY JACKSON

LAST Friday saw the new solo release from TONY JACKSON & THE VIBRATIONS, "Stage Door." The song, which was recorded at a session under the direction of ALAN FREEMAN, is, in Tony's opinion, the best he has released since leaving THE SEARCHERS.

Recently Tony completed a fortnight's tour of Scandinavia, where his previous disc, "Love Potion No. 9", reached the No. 9 position. During a break in rehearsals for A.B.C.'s "Thank Your Lucky Stars" he commented that the tour was one of his most successful yet and that he preferred Continental tours to any others.

"British audiences have reached saturation point. Even big name acts no longer draw the crowds. Everywhere we go, ballroom promoters tell us there has been a drop in attendances in recent months. I hate to say it, but the way things are going it looks as if the beat scene in Britain is dying.

"Of course, there are parts of England where name beat groups are still well received, but in London most teenagers just don't seem to want to know. One audience that is not yet blasé to pop stars is the Scottish. They at least react to a good stage presentation. You can always tell if an audience likes you. If, after two or three numbers, they don't respond, you

Tony Jackson

might as well give up.

"Records are, of course, the important thing. If you have a disc in the charts, the kids are more likely to sit up and take notice. If you haven't, well . . .

"Talking of records, I think there's a jinx on our recording sessions. We were to record with ANDREW OLDHAM, but at the last minute I fell ill with laryngitis. The session was postponed for two weeks, but when we came to record the number, Andrew had arranged it two notes lower than the key I was to sing it in. The deal to record under Oldham later fell through, so we recorded with ALAN FREEMAN, who I think is a first rate A & R man.

"There are very few really good recording managers. Oldham seems to be too carefree when recording. TONY HATCH, of Pye, is undoubtedly one of the best. When I was with THE SEARCHERS, he used to A & R our records and always sought perfection even if it took hours of re-takes. One thing I don't agree with at Pye studios is the way they dislike using electronic effects on a record. Now that I'm with THE VIBRATIONS we record independently for TITO BURNS at the Pye studios, which is in some ways better.

Surprised

"I was surprised at the reception when we played at the Grafton in Liverpool recently. We haven't played on Merseyside for some months and I suspected that the kids may have 'forgotten' about us. I'm glad to say that it was just the opposite and we played to a packed house."

Sandie on 'Scene'

Sandie Shaw appears on Granada-TV's "Scene At 6.30" next Thursday. Also booked are Tony Jackson and the Vibrations (Monday), Nashville Teens (Tuesday) and Herman's Hermits (Friday).

Below: Boredom taking its toll in TV studio dressing room

in Hamburg. The Star-Club in Hamburg was famous for The Beatles playing there before they became well known and it was a magnet for British bands. By this time Swenowa had left and Denis was driving the van and we set up our own equipment. It was too expensive to keep a roadie. It got harder to find work in England, so Germany was always a good place for gigs.

The Star-Club was a good gig for us and on the last night we doubled up with Johnny Gustafson (ex Merseybeats) for the last set which was really great.

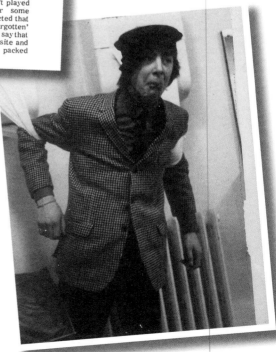

We had trips to Germany during the summer of 1965 and again in the spring, summer and autumn of 1966. The first occasion in July 1965 I was still only 17 and underage to work after 10 pm in Germany. I thought there was no way I was going to miss out again, so I changed the date of birth on my passport and dirtied it up a bit. I was always very nervous going through the passport checks. George Harrison had to return home when he was working there with The Beatles for being underage. Much later on I sent the passport back half burnt saying it had been in a fire. I received a new passport and I was OK again.

On our return we had a few gigs in Scotland. We did a couple and then Tony fell ill with his asthma and was in hospital. We played one gig without him and returned home. It was about this time that Tony split from Tito Burns and went with a chap called Mike Lescouli.

Es ist zu vermuten, daß Tony Jackson seinen vor etwas über einem Jahr gefaßten Entschluß, bei den Searchers als Sänger und Bassmann auszusteigen, inzwischen bereut hat. Seine hochgesteckten Erwartungen auf Plattenhits mit seiner neuen, eigenen Band (The Vibrations) haben sich nicht erfüllt. Inzwischen ist der Broterwerb für Tony, wie man hört, recht hart geworden.

THE HIT L.P. OF THE YEAR NPL 18108

PYE

SANDIE SHAW (THERE'S) ALWAYS SOMETHING THERE TO REMIND ME
THE KINKS YOU REALLY GOT ME
THE SHANGRI-LAS REMEMBER (WALKIN' IN THE SAND)
THE SEARCHERS WHEN YOU WALK IN THE ROOM
THE HONEYCOMBS HAVE I THE RIGHT
DIONNE WARWICK WALK ON BY
CHUCK BERRY NO PARTICULAR PLACE TO GO
THE DIXIECUPS CHAPEL OF LOVE
THE ROCKIN' BERRIES HE'S IN TOWN
KENNY BALL HELLO DOLLY
TONY JACKSON BYE BYE BABY
JULIE GRANT COME TO ME

THE HIT MAKERS

The fact is that Tito had done very well from the band because when we started gigging around the country we would often do two gigs in one night. We would set up and play for twenty minutes then drive to another venue about twenty miles away and do it all again. We were responsible for paying our own hotel bills out of our wages.

Tony also split from Pye and signed with CBS Records hoping for a new start and changed the band name to the Tony Jackson Group. Pye Records had brought out an LP and an EP called The Hit Makers and 'Bye, Bye Baby' was included on them.

Late 1965 we started to work on new recordings. Our producer was Irving Martin. We got on really well with him. We recorded our first single on the CBS label. This was a number called 'You're My Number One' and the B-side was a number called 'Let Me Know' written by Tony, Denis and Martin. This was released in January 1966. Again it received good air plays but did not get chart success.

THE TONY JACKSON GROUP

TONY JACKSON CUTS MOTOWN SOUND DISC

THE Tony Jackson group believe they have at last found the sound to put them into the top twenty. And it means a complete change from their recent discs, as they plan a full-blooded Tamla-Motown sound for their next release.

The news was broken to me by the group's drummer Paul Francis, only a few hours after an all-night recording session had ended.

"It was ridiculous (Paul's expression for fantastic). We never thought that 'Number One' was going to sell as many as it did because we didn't like the number but the record company say that it has sold over 9,000 and it's still selling.

"This means that we won't have a new disc out for a couple of months if the other one continues selling steadily.

"But," he added, "we think this new number is great, it's a Martha and the Vandellas song and we had three saxes, two trumpets and trombones, organ and piano on the session."

Last year the group had four singles released but just before Christmas they switched from Pye to C.B.S. and their organist Martin Raymond—second from right in our picture—left the group.

"We had planned to release another single quickly if the last record didn't hit the charts," Paul continued.

Plans for a double-A-side release have also been mentioned for their next disc. "But we've no idea what to make the B-side yet, so we'll have to wait and see."

Mike managed to get us regular work through January and February and we went back to the Star-Club in Hamburg in the spring.

The next A-side for CBS was a track called 'Never Leave Your Baby's Side' which Tony sang so well. We had a large brass section in the studio and I loved the full sound. The musical director was Des Champ, easy to get along with and very good at his job. The drum part I played was a pattern involving the toms which was not a problem to play but sounded better if I dubbed it on after and just played the first track straight. It worked a treat and is one of my favourite tracks which we recorded. I used a fill for the intro that also worked well. The B-side was a number called 'I'm The One She

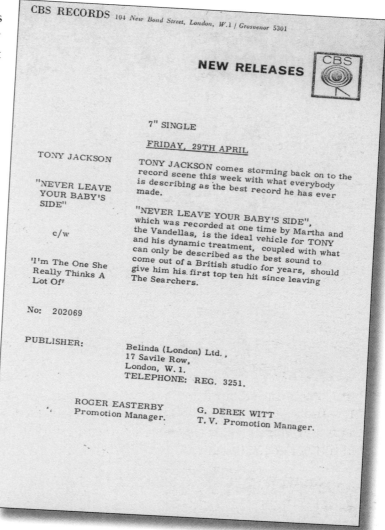

CBS RECORDS 104 New Bond Street, London, W.1 / Grosvenor 5301

NEW RELEASES CBS

7" SINGLE

FRIDAY, 29TH APRIL

TONY JACKSON

"NEVER LEAVE YOUR BABY'S SIDE"

c/w

'I'm The One She Really Thinks A Lot Of'

No: 202069

PUBLISHER:

TONY JACKSON comes storming back on to the record scene this week with what everybody is describing as the best record he has ever made.

"NEVER LEAVE YOUR BABY'S SIDE", which was recorded at one time by Martha and the Vandellas, is the ideal vehicle for TONY and his dynamic treatment, coupled with what can only be described as the best sound to come out of a British studio for years, should give him his first top ten hit since leaving The Searchers.

Belinda (London) Ltd.,
17 Savile Row,
London, W.1.
TELEPHONE: REG. 3251.

ROGER EASTERBY
Promotion Manager.

G. DEREK WITT
T.V. Promotion Manager.

Really Thinks A Lot Of' which was written by Ian, Tony and Martin. It sounded very much like a Beatles' track.

At the same sessions we also recorded 'Anything Else You Want' with the brass added. This was another number which had great vocals from Tony. This track was not released until November 1966 and the B-side was 'Come On and Stop'.

'Never Leave Your Baby's Side' was released in May 1966 and got a lot of airplays, especially on the pirate radio stations. It was very popular on Radio London and Radio Caroline. We did the ITV television show Five O'Clock Club. It was not a hit but it is a record I am very proud of. Irving had Tony's voice sounding great.

We also recorded the Beatles track "We Can Work It Out" but were advised that it was not single material and vocals were never added. The instrumental track was released some years later on a compilation record.

It was about this time that I started being used for sessions. Irving was passing quite a few on to me. I always enjoyed working in the studio. Sometimes a track would need extra toms or cymbals dubbed on, which meant an extra session fee. There was also a porterage fee. Let's face it drum kits are not the easiest instruments to get about. Flute players have it much easier!

One session at CBS in May 1966 was for Screaming Lord Sutch. It was an A-side called 'The Cheat'. The bass player on that session was John Paul Jones who later went on to play in Led Zeppelin. John did a lot of sessions as did Jimmy Page the guitarist. I enjoyed the Screaming Lord Sutch session; he was quite a character and a brilliant showman. The whole act was like Jack the Ripper with coffins on stage. It used to frighten the hell out of women. Tracks like 'I'm A Hog for You Baby' always went down well and a lot of bands included that number in their sets.

TONY Jackson is delighted with his latest disc "Never Leave Your Baby's Side." "I've more faith in this record than any other because of the tremendous interest C.B.S. have taken in me. They're genuinely helpful in every way—and I have quite a lot of promotion for the disc including 'Pick of The Pops,' 'Lucky Stars,' 'Five O'Clock Club' and 'Ready, Steady, Radio.' Apart from the group being on the record there are four saxes, trombone, piano, vibes, organ, tambourine and other instruments.

"Let's face it, three months ago things were bad as far as I was concerned. But I'm determined now because people have got faith in me.

"When I left the SEARCHERS it was easy to get a recording contract because people were interested in me. But we only had one hit—'Bye Bye Baby,' which got into the charts at 24—but we've been living on that one hit for two years. During that time I lost so much confidence performing-wise. At one time I used to feel great going on stage—but I think that feeling will return now that things are getting better.

"When you go through a bad spell like I have you feel that you're bashing your head against a brick wall. You make records which you consider to be good ones, but they don't do anything—and you notice records in the charts which are terrible and think that your lack of success is because people don't want to know you. It's made me very wary of people.

"I also get embarrassed with people—particularly members of 'in' groups who have got a superior attitude.

"In fact, one of the reasons I like to travel abroad for is that the attitudes are so different in foreign-speaking countries. They can't understand you so you don't get into so many fights. Over here there is always someone heckling. You can go into a pub for a quiet drink and you get the people making remarks about you.

"A while ago I began to feel like a boxer who has lost six fights and begins to lose his form . . . and reporters embarrass me when they ask the same old questions about 'what was it like being in the Searchers?'

"Now we've got a backer on the promoting side. If we need a new van or stage gear—we can get it. This makes us secure on the business side.

"I think the record is being released in about eight countries. In the States it's issued on the Date label and I may be going over there to promote the disc. Funnily enough, I'm still very well known over there—but kids keep sending me letters saying 'is it true you've left The Searchers?'

"What I really wanted when I left the group was to join another established group, so that I would be equal to the other members. I would have preferred that rather than starting from scratch. I would also have preferred people to look upon the group as four personalities, not one. When we play I try to push it that we are all equal—because I think that the other members are as important as I am. People watch me rather than the group and they miss things. IAN LEIGHTON is a great guitarist and drummer PAUL FRANCIS is only 18 but he does sessions with all the big session men—and he reads, too.

"As it is I have to carry the can and do everything. As leader, everyone looks to me to shoulder all the responsibilities.

"Apart from Ian and Paul, we have DENNIS THOMPSON on bass. Our organist MARTIN RAYMOND had to pack in because someone stole all our equipment, including the Vox organ he'd just bought—and he couldn't afford another one."

This week, Tony has an E.P. released in France: "The titles on it are 'Never Leave Your Baby's Side,' 'You're My No. 1,' 'Let Me Know' and 'I'm The One She Really Thinks A Lot Of.' We'll also be going over there for three days to promote it. We were originally going to go for three weeks but we had visa trouble. Then we go to Switzerland and have a tour of Germany after that."

How does Tony relax? "Well, I have a fairly quiet social life because I live out of town—about 15 miles outside of London. Also I'm usually so shattered with travelling round to different ballrooms that I just sit and watch T.V. or go to the movies."

TIME FOR A HIT FROM TONY

IT'S been quite a time since Tony Jackson was part of the hit-parade scene. Shortly after leaving The Searchers he had a minor hit with Love Potion No. 9, but since then, despite some good sounding discs, he has been absent from the charts.

But Tony—whose group contains two Barking boys—has obviously decided that it's about time he was back in the charts and with his latest disc a powerhouse version of Martha and the Vandellas "Never Leave Your Baby's Side" he seems all set to do just that.

But his group may feel a bit cheated by the release for though both Dennis Thompson and Paul Francis are on the disc only Tony is named on the label.

This is a pity for "Never Leave . . ." is undoubtedly the best disc Tony has made since he left the Searchers though the big-band backing tends to drown him slightly. Perhaps it is because of the change of style by using a brass section on the disc.

Bass guitarist Dennis told me that the flip side of the the disc "I'm the one she really thinks a lot of" sounds a bit like "She's A Woman". Which must rate as the understatement of the year. It's almost indentical to the Beatles' number but a nonetheless commercial effort.

All the group are waiting for now are the necessary television appearances. Already lined up is "Thank Your Lucky Stars"

Hard grind for Tony

BREAKING away from a world famous group to try to make it on your own can be tough. Ask Alan Price! He waited a year for a hit.

You can also ask Tony Jackson—or "Jake," as he was known to the Searchers in their hey-day of hits.

A year after he quit the top pop group, Tony said: "I'm glad I left the Search- ers. But you're still nobody without a hit!"

He found it a hard grind. Forming his own group, buy- ing them equipment and stage clothes, paying bills . . . it all came out of his personal savings. It came to a mammoth £2,000 in fact, "including £250 for my new nose," he grinned.

Today—not far off two years since he parted com- pany with the Searchers— things are at last looking up for Tony. His new single, the flip of a Martha and the Vandellas hit. "Never Leave Your Baby's Side," is sell- ing well.

Says Tony: "At last I'm alive again. I've been walk- ing round with my head down for too long. It's time things looked up."

Another one of my sessions was for a band called The Compromise on a number called "You Will Think of Me'. Tragically a few days later the singer was killed in a road accident.

We did an open air gig in Surrey where the organiser had catered for 250 people and about 3,000 turned up.

Towards the summer of 1966 the work in the U.K. was definitely drying up and it was now getting very costly for Tony to pay wages. We agreed that we would split the money from gigs and not take wages. This would help Tony. We needed to cut back expenses. In the past it had been good fun buying new shirts and clothes from Carnaby Street.

About this time I spoke to Eric Haydock who had quit The Hollies and was forming his own band Haydock's Rockhouse. Eric was keen for me to go to Manchester and have a try with the band. Dad took me up in the car. I felt guilty but thought I would have nothing to lose and I should at least see what Eric had to offer. Things had not been going so well with Tony.

When we arrived Eric showed me to a room upstairs above a pub. I was introduced to the rest of the band and we had a play. It sounded very good. Eric was always a good solid bass player. At the end Eric asked me to join and I said I would. However on the way home I thought about it and it would mean I would have to move to Manchester and all my family and friends were down south. I liked Manchester very much and always enjoyed playing there but I was not ready to move so on my return I contacted Eric and thanked him for the offer but declined the job. Eric went on to release a couple of singles with the band.

We went back to Germany in the summer of 1966. We often played at the Star-Club in Hamburg either headlining or as the house band. There were usually 3 bands each playing 45 minute sets throughout the night. The club opened at 4 p.m. and closed at 4 the next morning. If your band opened at 4 p.m. the next sets were 7 p.m., 11 p.m. and the last one was at 1 a.m. We got paid about £40 a week and the hotel expenses were met by the club.

During our wait between sets we would often sit in a small bar a few shops down from the Star-Club. You could get a good bowl of oxtail soup or a sausage. Horst was the owner. He had quite a reputation and nobody messed with him. The bands always gave him good business so he would look after us. We would also go to the Seaman's Mission which was good for cheap food.

tony jackson group

Right:
German
promotion card
Tony, Paul,
Denis, Ian

On one of our trips to Germany Tony and I swapped some shirts for two gas guns from a guy called Holly who was a fan of the band. They would fire gas pellets and blanks like a starting gun. We thought if we got any trouble we could fire it at the ground and the gas would make the attacker's eyes water for a while. Once in a hotel in England Tony fired his in the lift then got out. It went all over the hotel and the Manager asked us to leave. Everyone's eyes were watering. It was a silly thing to do.

Not long after the lift incident we were all piling into a waiting taxi when we were suddenly surrounded by very enthusiastic fans trying to grab hold of us. Once we were all in the taxi a man put his head through the open window next to Tony. He was shouting and obviously very excited. Tony ever quick to react took it as threatening behaviour and fired his gun which was loaded with blanks too close to the guy's face. The noise was deafening and we saw the guy's nose explode with the force because it was at close range; it was horrid.

We went to the hotel and the police arrived later on and questioned Tony about the incident. Tony pleaded self defence and I think they may have confiscated his gun and let him off with a caution. Tony regretted the incident but Tony was tough and would always stand his ground. Being a celebrity there is always someone ready to take a pop at you. I hid my gun and Grace told me years later that she had found it and got rid of it.

Also on one of our trips to the Star-Club The Luvvers (Lulu's backing group) were playing there   The drummer had a problem back home so I played with them for a week until he could join them.   I played a lot of sets that week!   The extra money was very handy.   During one visit I did a session with a band with lots of brass.   This was for a musician I had met who also did producing.   Again the extra money was great.

Another time in the gents toilets in a club in Germany, there was a man collecting a few pfennigs each time someone used the toilet.   He spoke good English and I felt sorry for him so I bought him a beer.   I told the other guys and they also bought him beers.   By the end of the night he was very merry.   He had a bald head with hair at the sides.   I got a lipstick from one of the girls and drew a face on his head.   The next night he was covered in cuts and bruises and we discovered that he had fallen into a ditch on the way home.   The face was still on his head!   I doubt he realised it was there.

During the summer of 1966 Tony and Martin were not getting on that well and Tony decided to drop the organ and just have a three piece backing him.   So Martin left.   It was not long before a chap called Ian Green helped out on Hammond Organ.   I loved the sound of the Hammond.   The Vox Continental which Martin played was OK but not a patch on the Hammond.   The only problem with a Hammond organ is getting the thing up stairs.   It took four of us to lift it.

Both Martin and Ian were good players.   Ian had a good knowledge of studio work. On gigs Ian would read everything which did not look the part on stage.   We arrived at a gig and because we were all so fed up with him reading the music I set fire to the parts so he had to learn the parts by ear!   Ian was not able to commit full-time to the band due to other work and he was not with the band very long.   He played on our next single 'Follow Me' and the B-side 'Walk That Walk'.

This was to be our very last recording on CBS in September 1966   Ian split the vocals with Tony and it sounded good.   There was a great Hammond organ on the B-side 'Walk That Walk' and really good vocals from Tony.   I liked the feel of that track and it is one of my favourite recordings along with 'Never Leave Your Baby's Side'.   'Follow Me' failed to chart.   By this time Tony had remarried and his wife Christine was expecting a baby.

Prior to one of our Star-Club visits we had a show in England with Johnny Kidd. Johnny had big hits with 'I'll Never Get Over You' and 'Shaking All Over'.   Shaking was a number one record.   Clem played drums and it was Clem's first number one hit.

After the show our van would not start.   Johnny very kindly offered us a lift back to London in his van.   We called at his house in the early hours of the morning for a cup

The man in the pop wilderness

TONY JACKSON is still without a hit record and it's more than two years since he vacated the bass players chair with the Searchers.

He has often said that he doesn't regret leaving the Searchers and at the moment they, too, are floundering in the pop wilderness.

Tony's failure to make a strong chart impression certainly cannot be attributed to any lapse on his part. He has fallen victim to that frequent disease "failing popularity".

Tony and his group have been in the wilderness for long enough and the extra fans they picked up with their last record "Never Leave Your Baby's Side", should stand them in good stead for a crack at the charts with their latest disc.

The group's reaction to "Fol- low Me" is not one of wild excitement. "It's all right," said Drummer Paul Francis, but he was hardly rapturous about its chances.

Clever harmonies, Beatle-ish backing and a strong vocal from Tony make this one of the group's best discs. The number was written by Bones Howe.

Flip-side "Walk, Walk, Walk" could be a number out of the James Brown show, very r and b slanted with guitar and organ prominent. C.B.S. is the label. It certainly stands a chance of making the top fifty.

of tea. His wife, Jean, made a brief appearance along with his lovely daughter who was only about five or six. She was so pleased to see her Daddy. We said our hellos and they both went back to bed. We had a good chat then made our way home.

Scene talk

The Tony Jackson group arrived back from the Star Club, Hamburg, on Wednesday after a three-week stint. Drummer Paul Francis sat in with the Luvvers' group who used to back Lulu. The group have had an offer of a trip to Poland

Sometime later while at the Pacific Hotel in Hamburg, Tony came into my room looking distressed. Upon enquiring what was wrong, he handed me The Express newspaper. Johnny Kidd had been killed on 7th October 1966 in a car crash. I could not believe it. It seemed like only yesterday we had been at his house. I felt so sorry for his wife and daughter.

Right:
Entrance to the Star-Club
Denis, Tony, Paul, Ian

81

How happy she was to see him when we were there and how nice his wife was. That hit us really hard. Johnny Kidd and The Pirates were a great band and well respected among all the musicians. It was a great loss.

Late autumn of 1966 we went to Karlsruhre, Germany for two weeks' work in the Star-Club there. We lived above the club in a couple of rooms with single beds. The windows were broken, it was awful. We thought the club owner would give us a little advance to tide us over but we were turned down. He told us he would pay us at the end of the week.

We pooled the cash and we only had enough for a doughnut each per day. We were starving. After three days we used to go back to bed in between sets to save energy. Then one night two American servicemen came to the club and we got talking to them. They liked the band and when they found out about our lack of food unbeknown to us they bought loads of hamburgers and we found them in our room on the radiator. They tasted fantastic. We could not believe what a nice thing it was to do for us. They were true friends. They came in most nights until we finished.

As there was no more work after that Tony went home by train and the band went to Hamburg. We travelled back to Hamburg in the van as the boys were keen to see their girlfriends. Denis had previously met Monika known as Peggy. We managed to get a weekend working at the Star-Club. John Wiggins an organist with the Big Six worked with us and we backed Paul Raven (later on known as Gary Glitter) who had been working in Germany for some time with the Boston Show Band.

Tony returned and we went to Kiel and Schleswig but the money was really poor. We returned to Hamburg and got a month working in the Star-Club finishing at the end of December. We worked through the night and slept during the day.

Christmas was quite good because all the groups were great guys. They were The Jackie Lomax Group (Jackie had previously been the lead singer with The Undertakers. He had a great voice.) and the Remo Four. We were all living on the fourth floor of the Hotel Pacific.

I remember one night trying to hail a cab to go back to the Pacific. Eventually one pulled up but it was full of people. They spoke English and asked where I was going. I told them and they said "Come with us, we are going to a party." I had nothing else to do so I got in and went with them. We arrived at the party and who should be there but Tony Sheridan, the singer who The Beatles had backed before they were well known. He was playing a really nice acoustic guitar.

Everyone was smoking dope and most were trying a hubble bubble water pipe. I had never tried one before so I thought I would give it a go. It was a bad move! Combined with the few beers I had consumed earlier the effect made me feel like crashing out. I found a room with a bed and fell asleep.

When I woke up it was all quiet. I opened the door and the room looked like a bomb had hit it. Things were smashed including the guitar Tony had been playing. I had obviously slept through a big argument for four hours! I could not believe it.

As we were finishing our month at the Star-Club Mike our manager informed us that we had work and a TV show in Madrid, Spain and we were to travel there from Hamburg. The atmosphere in the band was not great as Ian and Tony were at loggerheads and Ian threatened to leave. However, they managed to smooth things out and in early January we loaded up the van and we drove to Spain.

Christine and the baby were now travelling with us in the van along with Peggy from Germany who was Denis's girlfriend. It was a long journey and hot. Not the best

Long hair—so no TV show

THE Tony Jackson group arrived in Madrid last week ready to take part in a television show. But when they arrived at the studios the producer took one look at their long hair and cancelled the booking.

TONY JACKSON

"You should see the looks we get in the street," wrote drummer Paul Francis on a colourful postcard show-ing the Plaza de Cibeles y Pasco del Prado.

Spain is not noted for its tolerance of the long-haired set and a couple of years ago The Ricochets were ordered to get their hair cut while appearing at an American base in Spain.

The postcard also contained another surprise in that the group patched up the disagreement with lead guitarist Ian Leighton and he remains with the group.

This week they are recording and are expected to stay in Spain for two months.

TONY JACKSON GROUP
Vedetas do yé-yé Londrino de férias em Lisboa

UMA IMAGEM INSÓLITA: A DE UM CONJUNTO «POP» A ARRANCAR ESTRIDÊNCIAS DAS VIOLAS E DA BATERIA NO CENÁRIO DE UMA SALA DE «DÉCOR» PALACIANO, À LUZ DE LUSTRES, ENTRE PORCELANAS

of conditions to travel with a baby. It was not good for any of us. We finally arrived at our lodgings which was a pension (small hotel). Again we had very little money and would try to fill ourselves up with rolls at dinner. The work never materialised. We did one gig. The TV show did not happen as the producer took one look at our long hair and cancelled the booking.

We had no money to pay the pension bill so Denis arranged for his parents to send some money. The lady owner was really nice and Christine offered her wedding ring as collateral until the bill was paid.

While we were waiting for the money to arrive Ian had been in touch with his brother, Jimmy, who was in Lisbon, Portugal. Ian is half Portuguese and had family living there. Jimmy arranged some gigs for us in Portugal so once again we all piled into the van. On 22nd January we left Spain and travelled to Lisbon. Ian's cousin and family lived just outside Lisbon on the coast in Cascais so we based ourselves there. We kept the equipment in their games room and also did some rehearsals there. We played gigs at the Hotel Baia in Cascais and also at the local carnival dance.

We also had rehearsals in a beautiful house in Lisbon which was owned by another of Ian's cousins.   We did two shows at the Monumental Theatre and Cinema in Lisbon supporting Sylvie Vartan.

At the time both Spain and Portugal did not like men having long hair and on one occasion when we had publicity photos taken we had to sellotape our hair back as it was considered too long.

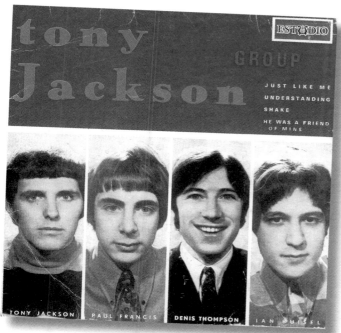

Jimmy's girlfriend had a connection with a radio station and recording studio.   We were meant to do a radio show but it was cancelled.   We managed to do a deal with them to record an EP in their studio while we were there.   We recorded four tracks.   'Just Like Me', 'Shake', 'He Was A Friend Of Mine', and 'Understanding' a Steve Marriot and Ronnie Lane song.   The recordings went well and it was released in the summer of 1967. This Estudio EP is very rare and sought after by Tony Jackson fans.

We had made just enough money to live on but had no money to get us home to England so we went to the British Embassy to get repatriated.

Tony, Christine and baby flew back to England and on 13th February we limped home in the van very disheartened.   We all knew it was the end.   The members of the band just went their own way.   There was no point in carrying on; the odds were stacked against us.   It was all very sad but it happens to bands all the time.   Some time later on there was an article in a daily paper saying Tony had taken a job on the railway.

The Searchers had a few more hits after Tony left but no more number ones. By the end of 1966 the hits had stopped. Mike Pender left a little later on to pursue a solo career which left The Searchers without their two lead vocalists. They carried on gigging with replacements but how can you replace the voices of Tony and Mike.   They were the sound of The Searchers.   It is a shame the band could not have settled their differences in the beginning then Tony and Mike could have shared lead vocals as Paul and John did in The Beatles.   Different tracks suited Paul taking lead and John on others.

I lost touch with Tony. Ian and I stayed in contact for several years. Tragically Ian died on 16th December 1987 after a stroke and brain haemorrhage. He was only 43. We all miss him very much. Ian was a very gifted guitarist and I loved his company. We had many laughs on the road and I am so pleased that at least he saw a little success before he died. His sister Marianna is a close friend. Denis married Peggy and they eventually went to live in America. I remained friends with them and his lovely family in Barking.

Twenty four years passed before I caught up with Tony with the idea of doing gigs again.

Chapter 4

Stuart James Inspiration/Pepper

Soon after the Vibrations broke up in March 1967 I took a job in a Soul band based in Chingford and London area. They were called The Stewart James Inspiration. No one in the band had that name but it sounded good.

I went for the audition at the The Swan in Tottenham. The band consisted of Roger Crisp on bass, Terry Clifford played guitar and Keith 'Nero' Gladman on vocals. They were former members of The Riot Squad one of the many bands associated with Joe Meek. Later on Keith told me they knew I was the drummer for them when they asked me if I wanted them to start and for me to come in and I told them I would count it in. The track was 'In The Midnight Hour' by Wilson Picket which has a distinctive fill at the beginning. Keith said as soon as I played they knew they need look no further. Keith had a real soulful voice and sang it great. I had always liked Soul and Motown music so I was pleased to get this gig.

Once I had joined we auditioned for brass players. Jimmy Jewell, who was a great player and had a mad sense of humour, came in on tenor sax followed by Larry Stubbins on baritone sax.

Again I was lucky as I moved in to lodge with Roger, his younger brother Brian and their parents. A really nice family. Roger's father, Roy, and a guy called Ivor Regan who ran a textile business in the East End were the managers of the band. We used a small van to travel to gigs.

We had hardly been together a few weeks when in April we went to Germany and played at the Liverpool Hoop Club in Berlin. Larry was not really fitting in with the rest of the band and after a couple of months he left and we recruited Bryn Collinson on baritone sax.

We had quite a bit of work but we needed to get some publicity so we started thinking of ways to get noticed. One idea was for me to try and break the World drumming record of 100 hours non-stop. I must have been mad. It was agreed that it would take place on 12th June 1967 at Tiles Club in London and someone had to be with me all the time to make sure I did not stop. I was fed by members of the band. Terry the guitarist was mainly on hand. When I visited the toilet I had to take a cymbal on a stand and keep playing. Very tricky!

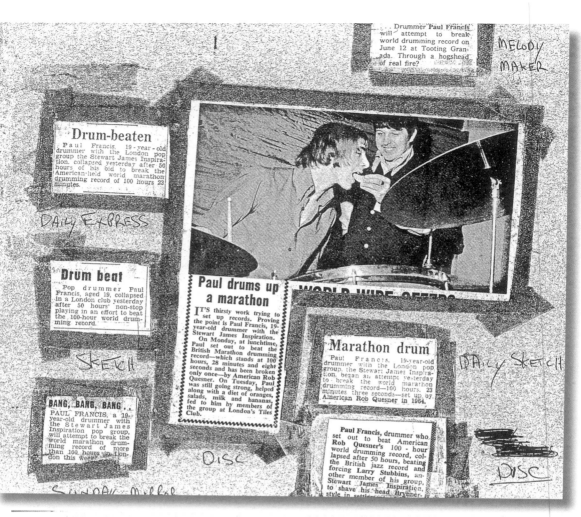

MELODY MAKER

Drummer Paul Francis will attempt to break world drumming record on June 12 at Tooting Granada. Through a hogshead of real fire?

Drum-beaten

Paul Francis, 19-year-old drummer with the London pop group the Stewart James Inspiration, collapsed yesterday after 50 hours of his bid to break the American-held world marathon drumming record of 100 hours 23 minutes.

DAILY EXPRESS

Drum beat

Pop drummer Paul Francis, aged 19, collapsed in a London club yesterday after 50 hours' non-stop playing in an effort to beat the 100-hour world drumming record.

SKETCH

BANG, BANG, BANG ...

PAUL FRANCIS, a 19-year-old drummer with the Stewart James Inspiration pop group, will attempt to break the world marathon drumming record of more than 100 hours in London this week.

SUNDAY MIRROR

Paul drums up a marathon

IT'S thirsty work trying to set up records. Proving the point is Paul Francis, 19-year-old drummer with the Stewart James Inspiration.

On Monday, at lunchtime, Paul set out to beat the British Marathon drumming record—which stands at 100 hours, 28 minutes and eight seconds and has been broken only once—by American Rob Quesner. On Tuesday, Paul was still going strong, helped along with a diet of oranges, salads, milk and bananas, fed to him by members of the group at London's Tiles Club.

DISC

Marathon drum

Paul Francis, 19-year-old drummer with the London pop group the Stewart James Inspiration, began an attempt yesterday to break the world marathon drumming record—100 hours, 23 minutes three seconds—set up by American Rob Quesner in 1964.

DAILY SKETCH

Paul Francis, drummer who set out to beat American Rob Quesner's 100-hour world drumming record, collapsed after 50 hours, beating the British jazz record and forcing Larry Stubbins, another member of his group, Stewart James Inspiration, to shave his head. Brynner-style in settle...

DISC

BRITISH CHAMP —AT DRUMMING

A Waltham Forest drummer set a British marathon drumming record last week — 50 hours non-stop.

Paul Francis, 19, of the Stewart James Inspiration, didn't even take the allowed breaks in beating the old record of 44 hours.

But he didn't starve.

Members of the group kept him supplied at Tiles Club, Oxford Street, with milk and bananas, oranges and salads.

Paul started at 1 p.m. June 12 but when he quit at 3 p.m. on June 14 he was still 50 hours 28 minutes, and eight seconds short of the world record, held by an American.

Manager Roy Crisp said: "We almost had to carry him out but the doctor says he's in perfect shape — just tired."

"He could have had breaks but he wanted it to be a real marathon.

Paul (extreme right) is pictured with other members of the group.   E67

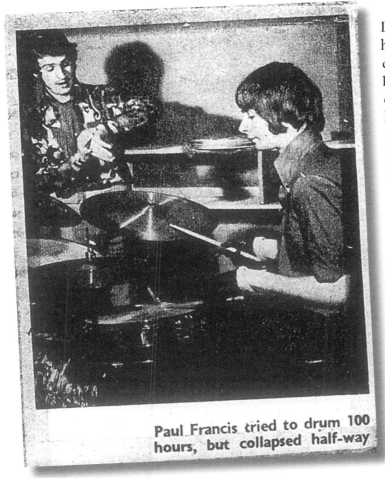

Paul Francis tried to drum 100 hours, but collapsed half-way

I managed to do about 50 hours without the aid of drugs but I just could not keep awake any longer. I did an interview for Jack de Manio on Radio 2 while still playing. A person would have to take something to keep them awake and I did not want to do that. Once I decided to stop my good old dad arrived and I went to stay in Kent for a few days. I fell asleep in the car. It was afternoon and the journey took about one and a half hours. I went straight to bed and did not wake up until late afternoon the next day. Boy, did I need that sleep.

When Mum came in she had the daily papers with her. There were pieces in The Sketch and Daily Express saying I had collapsed while trying to break the record. The Sketch had already put a piece in the previous day about my attempt at the record. The Sunday Mirror also put something in as did the music papers and various other papers. We were all pleased with the publicity as the band also had several mentions and photos.

I did not find the playing tiring at all; it was just the lack of sleep. Soon after that on 14th July we turned up at one venue, The Acorn Club, Bricket Wood, only to see a poster for the band with "featuring Paul Francis, British Drumming Record of 50 Hours" in bold print as large as the band name which really surprised me.

I left the Crisp family home and rented a small flat in Clapton. It had a kitchen and a room with two single beds in it. Bryn moved in with me to share the cost. I had a little practice pad kit in the kitchen which was always getting covered in cooking fat. There was a bathroom just outside our door but as we were at the top of the house we had it to ourselves. We later found out that this was the area where the Kray Twins used to hang out.

In the meantime Ivor had bought a coach. Our roadie, Mick Newing fitted the back half with a bed and bunks and left the seats in the front section. Having our own coach was brilliant. We all loved the coach, it was such good fun travelling in it. We used it to sleep in while we were away which saved money on hotels as we played a lot of gigs up and down the country. It had a big double bed at the rear which Roger claimed. It made sense as he was much bigger than the rest of us.

The band was popular at all the venues where we played. We even took part in an advert for Kent cigarettes where we were playing in a club. It was fun seeing it on the big screen in the cinema.

While playing out of London one night, I noticed a small motor bike for sale. It was very old but I took a fancy to it and bought it. We had a friend called Roe with us at the venue who said he would ride it back and follow the van. The bike was left in the front garden, but I never did use it. It eventually got stolen. Not long after that Roe was killed in a road accident. Such a shame, he was a really nice man.

It was time to cut a single. At the same time we changed the group name to Pepper. On 28th April 1968 I was back again in good old Pye Studios. This time we used the smaller studio.

Above from left to right: Jim, Terry, Nero, Roger, Paul, Bryn

90

An Australian band called The Easy Beats had a hit in England with 'Friday On My Mind', a good song. Vanda and Young, two members of the band who wrote their material, offered us two of their songs. The A-side was 'We'll Make It Together' which was a ballad coupled with 'Look Out I'm On The Way Down' on the B-side. Alan A. Freeman was the producer and he was taken ill for a week during the recordings. Nero sang both songs really well and we were pleased with the backing. The Breakaways sang the backing vocals. I think I preferred the B-side. The record was released on 19th July but never received huge air plays so did not do anything chart-wise.

We played a gig near Sheffield and the support band was Joe Cocker and The Grease Band. They were completely unknown at that time. We heard their sound check and were blown away by them. Such a tight band with Joe's amazing vocals. During their set they played the Beatles song 'With A Little Help From My Friends'. We could not believe what we were hearing. The arrangement and Joe's vocals sounded fantastic. When they came back to the dressing room we told them they should record that version as it would be a hit. I am so pleased they did. It was a massive hit for them in November 1968. Joe had air plays with his first single but it was 'A Little Help' which really made it for him.

It was about this time that I met my wife, Goldie, which is short for Goldina. She was named after her paternal grandmother who had the name given to her from the gold rushes in America. Goldie knew Mick, our roadie, and he told her about the band. They came to a couple of gigs and called in one day to see Bryn and me. Goldie lived in Chelmsford. I thought she was gorgeous and fell for her straight away. We started dating.

Jim had been trying to get me to move in to a large house where he was staying in Liverpool Road, Islington. He said I could use his room as he was always staying with his girlfriend. Keith was the landlord and Martin, a friend of Jim also lodged there. Martin's room was right at the top of the house. We used to collect Jim from the house on our way to gigs and one day I asked Martin to come to the gig with us as he seemed at a loose end. He thought about it then said no, he'd give it a miss this time. Martin also played guitar, so he was into music. We said goodbye and went to the gig. We dropped Jim off at his girlfriend's on the way home. The next day Jim went back to the house and could not get a reply from Martin. There was a smell of gas. Jim managed to get into Martin's room to find he had committed suicide. He had left the gas on and put towels under the door. He left a suicide note addressed to Jim.

Poor Jim, it was a terrible thing to happen and to be the first person to find him. Very upsetting. After a while Jim mentioned that Martin's room was free. I said there was no way I was using that room. So Keith changed rooms; he had Martin's and I took

Keith's. We all shared a tiny kitchen, about six feet by four feet upstairs at the top of the house, and a bathroom on the landing. But it was fine, we lived on beans and eggs most of the time, plus takeaway Chinese. They got to know us well there.

There was a large lounge at the front of the house on the first floor and Keith said I could put my drums in there and use it to practice in. I would do eight hours a day for two weeks then cut back to four hours for a while then back to eight hours. If I started early it gave me the evenings free to go out. I really enjoyed the discipline and it paid off as my technique improved. There is no short cut to playing a musical instrument well. You only get out what you are prepared to put in. Drumming to me is not about playing really fast all the time, but to develop speed you have to work at it slowly. Too many students are not prepared to do that.

I must admit I did not like being on my own in the house after what happened to Martin. I would leave lights on when I went to bed. As a young child mum and dad would leave the bathroom light on for a while when I went to bed as it shone through the window above my door. Even now I like some light in the bedroom and rarely have the small window closed and the curtains fully drawn.

Chris Spedding, the guitarist who had a hit with 'Motor Biking' in 1975, had a room on the top floor. Later on I played on one of his tracks 'Don't Leave Me' on his 1972 album 'The Only Lick I Know'. Chris played in a dance band to start with and went on to work with many top artists including Paul McCartney. Chris, Henry Lowther on trumpet, Jim on Sax and I used to have jam sessions with a bass player called Butch. These took part in the front lounge. There was a lovely old couple living next door and I would always ask if it annoyed them but they said they liked to hear the music.

After about a year the band was not really going anywhere. We had a few weeks' work in Germany lined up so we decided we would do that then go our own ways. It was at this time at the end of July 1968 that I received a phone call from Chris Dreja saying my name had been put forward for the New Yardbirds and was I interested. The Yardbirds were parting and this was a new group with Jimmy Page and Chris. I said I was but I had two weeks' work in Munich to finish. He said that he would contact Jimmy and when I returned we would have a get together and see how it sounded.

Pepper embarked on their final German tour. It was all very civil and we had a great time. We played in Berlin and Munich. There was a lot of construction work going on in Munich as they had started building the stadium for the Olympics four years later in 1972.

We played at The Blow Up Club in Munich and the lodgings where we stayed had two big rooms off a courtyard. The English band which had stayed there before us had left without paying and the landlady was trying to get us to pay for them. She thought that we must know them as we were both English and played at the same club. We thought stuff that it was nothing to do with us.

On our final night we left a small amount of money for her and we all sneaked out into the van leaving poor Keith to check the rooms then leave. He drove like mad. We all thought we were going to get stopped before we made it to the border!

On our return Chris Dreja and I spoke again and he said that he was having trouble getting hold of Jimmy. He was a difficult person to pin down. That was as far as it went and I heard no more. Much later on I found out that Chris had decided to leave the band.

Over the years there have been several books about The Yardbirds and Led Zeppelin stating that myself, B. J. Wilson, Clem Cattini and Aynsley Dunbar were being considered for the gig. One even said that I had joined and we were to tour Scandinavia, which was quite amusing. It was a bit like Chinese Whispers where things get exaggerated. In 2010 I did an interview with Barney Hoskyns who was writing a book about Led Zeppelin and I gave him the true account of my involvement.

Pepper broke up the end of August and we went our separate ways. Jimmy Jewell joined Keef Hartley Band and later on played with McGuinness Flint, Ronnie Lane & Slim Chance and Gallagher & Lyle.

Chapter 5

The End/Tucky Buzzard

I had already made contact with a band called The End who were produced by Bill Wyman and were looking for a drummer. Hugh Attwooll their drummer had decided to quit and stay in Spain where the climate suited his asthma better than Britain. The End had done quite a lot of work over there. I auditioned for them in a basement studio in Bermondsey which was owned by The Rolling Stones. It went very well and I joined The End. The End had already had tracks released by Decca in the UK.

This whole set up seemed very professional. The music was more rock orientated and it made a change from the soul music; a new challenge. The studio was great, quite large so plenty of room. Other acts also used it. We once met Janis Joplin there and had a good chat with her. She was really nice. Ian Stewart, the Stones' road manager and keyboard player, used to run it. It was mainly used as a rehearsal studio.

Nicky Graham played keyboards with The End. We would often do some rehearsals at his house. Dave Brown was on bass and Terry Taylor played guitar. The End had used John Horton and Gordie Smith on saxes in their previous line up and Colin Giffin had played guitar and done vocals.

Left:
The End 1968
Paul, Nicky,
Dave, Terry

We went to Spain in December 1968 and played in various clubs including JJs and Picadilly in Madrid. We played some of the early Led Zeppelin tracks as well as our own numbers. (The New Yardbirds had by now turned into Led Zeppelin). The bands in Spain were years behind; they were still playing 'Black Is Black' by Los Bravos. We built up a good following of musicians wanting to check us out. I enjoyed playing the clubs.

We stayed in pensions which were in between a hotel and a guesthouse. We would eat at a small cheap café nicknamed the Greasy Spoon where the owner and the waiter were like a cabaret act. The young one could hardly write and the older one would always have to check what he was doing and often clipped him round the head. It was a forerunner of Fawlty Towers. We would fall about laughing. Dave and I both had a sweet tooth and would always try to outdo each other on the dessert. Usually it was strawberries and cream on the menu. We would see who could manage to order the most unusual. Once I ordered just a bowl of cream which really made Dave laugh.

We had been offered work over the New Year in a ski resort called Font-Romeu-Odeillo-Via in the Pyrenees near the border of France and Spain. We would be there to see in the New Year. A friend called Rob would drive us and his friend, Malcolm, who had just had a nasty car accident, would come along for a break.

We were all really tired. It had been a long journey. All the equipment was in the back of the van behind a partition. I was in the back seat with Dave sitting next to me. He had his coat over his head trying to sleep! We were up in the mountains. Rob cut a corner leading to a bridge over a river and was a little way over in the lane of oncoming vehicles. The only problem was the driver coming the other way had also cut the corner. Both vehicles finished up on the wrong side of the road to avoid a head on crash. We struck the bridge and the van toppled over into a small river. Not another damned bridge. This was getting to be a regular occurrence. Fortunately the river was only about a foot deep but everyone fell backwards onto the passengers in the back of the van. Dave still had his coat over his head. It was dark and I could smell petrol. I thought the van might go up. It was very frightening.

The driver of the other vehicle ran back and was trying to pull Rob out only he still had his seat belt on. Some of our paperwork and belongings were washed away. We eventually climbed out and got onto the road, wet and shaken. Dave and I had a fit of giggles much to the annoyance of Nicky. I think it was the shock coming out but it could also have been helped by a certain substance in which we had indulged to ease the boredom of the journey. Someone said the van was a write-off by the look of it and we had no idea what state the equipment was in. Goodness, now we were in the shit!

Someone managed to get to a phone and after a while two old-fashioned Citroen estate cars arrived. We managed to get into the back of the van and luckily because the equipment had been packed really tightly it seemed to be OK. The water had not done too much damage. The amp valves were bound to need replacing. We loaded the equipment into the vehicles and went on to the resort.

Poor Malcolm who had come with us to recover from an accident looked shaken and had cuts to his nose. This set Dave and I off giggling again. Malcolm was trying to see the funny side but was still in shock. Dave and I were trying to make light of it and take his mind off the situation. We were so relieved to get to the ski resort and find our accommodation.

The next day we telephoned home to get another van and driver. Luckily our friend Rod Duncan said he would bring one out. Several days later Rod arrived with a van. It was great to see him, plus a big relief to get another van. Rod stayed for a day then returned home. The shows went OK. We tried to play music that they were familiar with as well as our own.

From the Pyrenees we went back to Madrid for a further three weeks work and then back to the U.K. It was good to get back home again and start working on new songs. Bill was still trying to get The End a record deal in America.

We started to put down tracks at Olympic Studios in Barnes, which sadly closed in 2009. Practically every band had used Olympic. There was one very large studio and a smaller one. The Stones, Small Faces and Led Zeppelin all used Olympic. Carrying my kit in one day I opened the studio door to find all four members of The Beatles standing round the piano. That took me by surprise as I was not expecting anyone to be in there.

I really loved recording at Olympic. We always got a good sound and Bill did a great job with the production. I was now using a Ludwig kit. Many players switched to Ludwig after Ringo starting using them. They are an American company. My kit had two toms. The sessions were mostly at night finishing in the early hours of the morning and were spread out over a good part of a year.

The End only did one or two gigs in England, most of the work was in Spain. We also started to back Billie Davis, who had a big hit with a track called 'Tell Him'. Billie was very easy to work with and we got on well with her and her husband Alan, who was also her manager. She was very popular in Spain and we did quite a lot of work there in clubs and bullrings. The gigs were very handy for us and it was nice playing different material. We also played a gig in Jersey with her.

Towards the end of April 1969 we went to Hamburg. I was to play at the Star-Club again. We really enjoyed ourselves there; we had good fun with the other bands. Black Sabbath with Ozzy Osbourne were on only they were called Earth then. Another band called The Ace Kefford Set were also on. Ace was a former member of The Move.

Above:
The End with Billie Davis. Malaga Bullring, Spain. Autumn 1969

Bands would start playing about four o'clock in the afternoon and play for about 45 minutes, then the next band would take over. This would continue until closing time around 4 in the morning. A lot of jamming went on with various musicians sitting in with other bands. On one occasion for the final few hours it was agreed that all three bands, us, Ace and his band plus Ozzy and the boys would have one big jam. It was great. Ozzy enjoyed himself and I had a ball. The drummer for Ace was Cozy Powell and Bill Ward was the drummer for Ozzy and Earth. It was such a monster sound with all the instruments playing. You can imagine three drummers going for it. Bill Ward and Cozy Powell were great players, so I had a blast playing with them. It was a great way to finish the night. Cozy Powell went on to have great success with many well-known bands and as a solo artist. Unfortunately he was killed in a car crash in 1998, aged just 50.

Ozzy and the band never seemed to sleep. If we were really tired we would take a pill called a Purple Heart that would do the job and keep us going. However you could also not stop talking. But you felt rough once it had worn off.

Most of the musicians bought leather jackets from the local market called the Fish Market which sold most things. The jackets were second hand, ex-Police I think and they were cheap. Poor Ozzy had his stolen along with some money in the pocket from their dressing room.

When we made our way back to the Pacific Hotel in the early hours of the morning various clubs had men dressed as women standing in the doorways trying to encourage drunken sailors to enter. The only problem was they had a day's growth of beard! Nothing surprised you in Hamburg.

We returned to the U.K. in June but left the end of July to go to Spain for more work and we stayed out there for quite a few months.

On one of our trips to Spain when we were playing at a sports arena in Barcelona, Dave and I decided we needed to have a hair cut; not short but tidied up a bit. We checked out the best hairdressers and booked an appointment the day before the gig. The man did a good job on our hair and in conversation asked what we were doing in Barcelona. As soon as he heard that we were musicians he asked if we would like to go to a party for Salvador Dali that evening at the Hotel Ritz. Of course, we said yes that would be great.

Dave and I turned up that evening and made our way upstairs to a large suite being used for the party. Dali had a huge entourage of people around him. He looked over to where Dave and I were standing and came straight over for a chat ignoring everyone else. He asked us what we did and we told him about the gig at the sports arena. Dali said we were all artists, and to our surprise he said he would come to the gig, saying "Dali will come." It was a great honour to have met him.

The next day Dave and I told the others what had happened. We really did not expect him to turn up, but blow me down he was good to his word and there he was. Dave had a better view from the stage as I was at the back on the drums. He said as Dali walked in the audience parted to let him through. It was great for all of us.

Dali lived a couple of hours north of Barcelona and would book a suite at the Ritz when in town. He would also book a suite for his paper mache horse. What a fantastic story. I enjoyed meeting him very much. He was a great artist.

The band somehow or other got involved in doing a bit part in a film being shot in Madrid. We were friends with a well-known disc jockey and I think he put a word in for us. The film was called 'Un, Dos, Tres, Al Escondite Ingles' and was screened at the Cannes Film Festival in 1970. Nicky flew back to Spain for the premier. Many years later I managed to get a DVD copy of the film.

We also made friends with a Spanish singer called Miguel Rios. He was very popular and was the Spanish equivalent to Cliff Richard. He really liked the band and we backed him once augmenting his own band. Miguel had many hits in Spain so again it was getting the band noticed. He asked if we would back him on his new LP and he wanted to do some of our original numbers. He really liked one track called 'Second Glance'. This was to be the title track translated into Spanish as 'Despierta'.

During that trip I managed to see Joe Morello do a drum clinic on 11th November 1969. I have always liked his playing especially on the Dave Brubeck track 'Take Five'. After the clinic people were queuing for autographs so I thought I would too. When I spoke he sounded so pleased to hear an English accent and he asked what I was doing in Spain. He was genuinely interested to hear about the gigs and recording. Joe continued teaching in America until his death in March 2011. A great player and teacher.

So in January 1970 we returned to Madrid to record with Miguel. We played on several tracks including a version of Elvis's 'Jailhouse Rock'. This was released as a single in Spain as 'Rock de la Carcel' and reached number 5 in the charts. 'Despierta' was the B-side. Miguel also had a big hit with 'Song of Joy' which was taken from Beethoven's 9th Symphony with added lyrics. It was a hit in many countries around the world including the UK.

On the strength of that LP, Hispavox, the record label, asked The End to do an album on our own. Their studio in Madrid was massive and had a really good sound. We signed contracts and agreed to come back and do the album a few months later.

We were lucky to get the amount of work we did in Spain as things in England were slow to get off the ground. We grabbed any studio time available at Olympic Studios to try and get as many tracks down as possible. Various members of the Stones would pass by from time-to-time to have a listen. Mick Taylor the Stones' guitarist played guitar on a couple of tracks.

Goldie and I got to see the Stones play a couple of times. The first time was with the rest of Tucky Buzzard at The Round House on 14th March 1971 just before they departed to live in France. The other time was at Wembley Arena. We met Bill and Astrid at the Dukes

HIT disco expres

35 EXITOS DE LA SEMANA

6th JUNE 1970

(VOTOS DE LOS LECTORES)

SEMANA ANTERIOR / SEMANAS EN LISTA / PUESTO MAS ALTO

			SEMANAS EN LISTA	PUESTO MAS ALTO
1.	(3)	PUENTE SOBRE AGUAS TURBULENTAS ... Simon y Garfunkel	(11)	(1)
2.	(1)	JINGO ... Santana	(8)	(1)
3.	(2)	LET IT BE ... Beatles	(14)	(1)
4.	(9)	SI LA MUERTE PISA MI HUERTO-COMO UN GORRION ... Serrat	(5)	(4)
5.	(11)	ROCK DE LA CARCEL/DESPIERTA ... Miguel Ríos	(4)	(5)
6.	(13)	UN RAYO DE SOL ... Diablos	(4)	(6)
7.	(5)	SOY UN HOMBRE ... Chicago	(9)	(5)
8.	(8)	CORPIÑO XEITOSO ... Andrés do Barro	(6)	(7)
9.	(7)	TRAVELING BAND ... Creedence Clearwater Revival	(10)	(7)
10.	(4)	GWENDOLYNE ... Julio Iglesias	(11)	(1)
11.	(10)	INSTANT KARMA ... John Ono Lennon	(7)	(6)
12.	(14)	SPINNING WHEEL ... Blood Sweat and Tears	(7)	(7)
13.	(22)	CECILIA ... Simon y Garfunkel	(3)	(13)
14.	(12)	POETAS ANDALUCES ... Aguaviva	(18)	(4)
15.	(23)	IO IO ... Bee Gees	(3)	(15)
16.	(16)	ESTRELLA ERRANTE ... Lee Marvin	(8)	(12)
17.	(25)	LA CASA DEL SOL NACIENTE ... Frijid Pink	(3)	(17)
18.	(6)	COLORES ... Karina	(10)	(5)
19.	(15)	MUCHISIMO AMOR ... Led Zeppelin	(19)	(1)
20.	(17)	VIVE LA REALIDAD ... Brincos	(6)	(17)
21.	(19)	TRABAJEMOS JUNTOS ... Canned Heat	(6)	(18)
22.	(30)	LA CIUDAD DE LA LUZ/MANZANAS AZULES ... Valen	(2)	(22)
23.	(18)	TOC TOC ¿QUIEN HAY? ... Mary Hopkin	(7)	(15)
24.	(31)	ESPIRITU EN EL CIELO ... Norman Greenbaum	(2)	(24)
25.	(32)	SUNDAY MORNING ... Oliver	(2)	(25)
26.	(28)	SENTIMENTAL GIRL ... Jackie	(12)	(16)
27.	(34)	ALELUYA DEL SILENCIO ... Raphael	(2)	(27)
28.	(21)	QUE TE QUIERO ... Mike Kennedy	(13)	(5)
29.	(24)	THE RAPPER ... Jaggerz	(5)	(24)
30.	(20)	JENNY ARTICHOKE ... Fórmula V	(8)	(12)
31.	(—)	SEÑOR DOCTOR ... Payos	(1)	(31)
32.	(—)	LYLA ... Lone Star	(1)	(32)
33.	(26)	MONICA ... Angeles	(16)	(7)
34.	(—)	EL AGUILA DE LA MUERTE ... Cerebrum	(1)	(34)
35.	(27)	ROOM TO MOVE ... John Mayall	(6)	(21)

SINGLE IN THE CHARTS IN SPAIN 1970

Hotel where they were staying, then we went to the show together. I can remember the light show being amazing. There was a row of white lights shining upwards across the back of the stage which produced a fantastic effect. The Arena is a good-sized venue to see bands. I always think the bigger venues with video screens lose the atmosphere.

I loved my time with the band but there were months with nothing going on with no money coming in. I found that frustrating. Our big aim was to get to America. I had never been there. About this time it was decided that perhaps we should have a lead vocalist in the band. Nicky was doing a good job but he was seated at the keyboards. Likewise Dave had a good voice but he was playing bass. A front man would be visually better. Terry suggested Jim Henderson, a vocalist he had previously worked with.

Jim came along and fitted in really well, so we had to get him rehearsed and up to scratch. All new songs would have Jim on vocals. He also wrote lyrics which was good for new material.

101

My wedding was looming up. My brother, Geoff, was away on a long tour with the Navy so could not be my Best Man. Keith, my landlord and now a friend, agreed to take the role. I thought as he was an actor he would be ideal. We were getting married on Saturday 4th April 1970 at Widford Church, Chelmsford, and the reception was at The County Hotel.

I bought my first suit, a dark red tweedy number, and Keith worked on his speech. Keith and I travelled to Chelmsford on the day by train and had a taxi to the church. It was a freezing cold day with wind and rain. Goldie looked fantastic. She was given away by her dad and was attended by her cousins Vanessa, 15, and Sara nearly 5, and Geoff's twins, Wayne and Julie, 5. Goldie wore a white dress and the bridesmaids and page boy wore lilac and purple velvet. The service went well, but once outside it was blowing a gale. Guests were huddled together; Goldie's veil was blowing sideways and my hair joined it! It was decided that photos would be taken at the Reception.

We had about a hundred guests including members of Pepper, The End and partners and Bill Wyman and Astrid. Keith did not drink as a rule but when he did it would go straight to his head. We had sparkling white wine and when it came to his turn he stood up, said one sentence and sat down again. It was very funny, but at least there was no long drawn out best man's speech. After the reception guests were invited back to Goldie's parents' house. A lot of people came back including Bill and Astrid. His Mercedes with darkened windows was certainly a talking point.

Bill asked us up to Gedding in Suffolk to stay for a few days. Gedding is such a lovely house. It was very relaxing after all the running around leading up to the wedding. Bill has so many silver and gold discs. On seeing them I remarked that I would love to have one. Bill told me that I could have one of his. I thanked him and declined the offer as it would only really mean something if I had earned it myself. What a generous offer from Bill though. He said he thought it was a shame that he had so many yet musicians like me had none. I told him he deserved them as he had worked hard to get them.

Three weeks after the wedding on 25th April the band went to Spain to start recording at Hispovox. Goldie came with me which was nice and we took her car instead of travelling in the van. The ferry crossing to Bilboa was quite rough and nearly everyone was seasick. We stayed in Bilboa where we bumped into the band Affinity. Mo Foster, Lynton Naiff and Linda Hoyle were covered in bites from bedbugs and they warned us about cheap pensions not being very clean.

We went to Madrid and stayed in a pension. However, the studio was not ready for us and we were sitting around doing nothing for weeks. We played a lot of Monopoly and some of us were better losers than others.   It was a tough time, especially for Goldie and me as this was our first taste of living together.   Not really the rock star's life I would have liked to show her.   We had the equivalent of 50p a day to live on. Fortunately we had friends in Madrid, including Hugh, The End's previous drummer. He and I became good friends and we spent time with him and Marian his girlfriend.

The band was offered two weeks' work at the new Hotel Don Toni, Playa den Bossa, Ibiza. When we arrived we found the hotel was incomplete. The manager told us there would be a slight delay until we started playing but to enjoy the stay in the meantime. The hotel was right on the beach so everyday we would go swimming and sunbathing, sometimes we would go into the old town, but we had so little money we were limited to what we could do.

We had all our meals at the hotel but we were counted as staff and the room where we ate was open to the elements; the outside wall was missing! It was always full of flies. We eventually started playing in the nightclub downstairs but there were not many guests. We finished up playing Wes Montgomery numbers as we knew the manager liked him. We stayed there about 6 weeks in all; we were all very tanned and very poor.

Towards the end of August we headed back to Madrid and then on to England.   Jim and his girlfriend Cathy travelled back with us in the car. We had two days to make the ferry. We broke down in the middle of Spain and spent the night on the floor of a small room at a service station. The car was fixed and we were on our way.   Driving through France we stopped for fuel and as we got down the road, we realised that we should have had more change so we had to go back and retrieve it, which was not easy as non of us spoke much French. Because we had so little money we knew exactly how much we needed to get home.   We took a Spanish slimming drug to help us keep awake for the non-stop journey.   We arrived home on 20th August 1970.

The band went back to Madrid a couple of months later and started recording.   This time we rented a large apartment which was perfect for us. We would start recording about nine in the morning and finish about six or seven.   We would return to the apartment, cook a meal and have a few beers and relax. It worked really well.

The recording went well. On one number I used tymps and a full orchestra was added later.   One side of the album had each song running into the next which worked well. Hugh came and played bongos and Len Neldrett, a guitarist friend living in Madrid, played some guitar. It was good catching up with them again and also Charlie Mendez who was Spanish and a real fan of the band.   Hugh had a really good command of the language by now.   There were a lot of English musicians working in Spain; Chris Johnson and Ian Hague were two drummers we bumped into a lot.

Whilst in the studio we also recorded a Mungo Jerry hit called 'In The Summertime'. We released it as 'En el Verano' under a different name 'Polos Opuestos' as it was not our style. A number written by the band called 'Smarty Pants' was on the B-side.

On returning home we fitted any spare time we could in the studio putting down new tracks. Various people were trying to get the band a deal in America and Bill was in talks with them

Pepper had gigged all the time. It was different with The End as more time was spent in the studio which was great but apart from Spain and Germany it was very quiet gig-wise. I found that frustrating; I think we all did. Towards the end of 1970 we played at The Pheasantry in Kings Road and Maximus in Leicester Square a few times.

The Spanish LP was released in 1971. It was fantastic hearing it finished especially with the full orchestra. I have always loved strings. Dave was such a good song writer and his voice was quite distinctive when he took lead vocals. Waldo de los Rios was responsible for the orchestral arrangement and he did a great job. Rafael Trabucchelli produced the LP along with a big input by the band. All the material was written by the band. Terry played lovely acoustic guitar on 'Maryse' which was a piece dedicated to his daughter. Terry was excellent at classical pieces and would often play some for me when we were in hotels.

Everyone played so well on that LP and it had been a joy to record. Plus having our bit all finished in a week was good going. The LP was well received in Spain. It was released in the UK much later. Earlier in 1970 about the time Jim had joined we had decided to change the band name and we were called Tucky Buzzard. I'm not sure how the name came about but we all agreed on it. The album was called 'Coming On Again'.

From back left to right:
Dave Brown & Gwyneth, John Horton,
Nicky Graham, Terry Taylor,
Gordon Smith, Colin Giffin,
Miguel Rios, Bill Wyman,
Hugh Attwooll, Paul Francis.
Padstow, 5th October 1991

I joined the band in 1968 and it was now coming up to Christmas 1970 and still no record deal and no money coming in. I was starting to feel disillusioned and did not want to start another New Year in this way. Bill was doing all he could to get a deal but it was in the hands of others.

One day I received a phone call from Graham White, a guitarist, telling me about a new band he was putting together and asked if I was interested. The band would be managed by Gordon Mills who handled artists such as Tom Jones, Englebert Humperdink and Gilbert O'Sullivan. Gordon wanted a heavy rock band on his new MAM record label. Graham said he had Roy Sharland on keyboards and Mick Hawksworth on bass, he just needed a drummer. He came round to have a chat. I was in a real quandary about what I should do. I loved Tucky Buzzard and all the guys, but it was frustrating with nothing happening.

Chapter 6

Fuzzy Duck, Bill Wyman and John Walker

Graham was aware of my playing and so there was no audition. The job was mine if I wanted it. This was not an easy decision for me. Apart from the music, Dave and I were good friends and we had so many laughs together. He was also a great bass player to work with.

Gordon Mills at that time had the Midas Touch. He was having so much success. This could be a good career move, so I decided to quit Tucky Buzzard. On New Year's Eve I called the guys and told them; they understood about it. Word got to Bill and he called me from abroad to have a chat. The record deal was talked about but I think even Bill was getting impatient with Capital Records. He fully understood my feelings and wished me well. The band contacted Chris Johnson in Spain to take my place. They would have someone they knew and Chris fitted in well. I did the last gig with them on 14th January 1971 at The Pheasantry.

The album that we had been working on called 'Tucky Buzzard' was eventually released in 1971 containing seven tracks with me playing and three with Chris. The vocals had been split between Nicky, Jim and Dave taking the lead, with Terry on backing vocals. It was great to hear it again but I must say the album cover looked like it had been put together in five minutes. However, the tracks sounded great and Bill had done a good job.

The band eventually made it to America and I would have loved to have been there with them. I was very pleased for them, but I had made my decision. We all kept in touch. When they split up Jim went to America and Dave worked in A & R for Polydor and eventually settled in Cornwall. Nicky became a producer and had success with the duo Bros. Terry worked for Bill and played in Bill's band The Rhythm Kings.

It was time to get things started with the new band. We met up and all got on very well. We started rehearsing and met Gordon Mills. Gordon was a no messing man; get the job done and that's it. Geoffrey Everitt was looking after the band at MAM, Gordon's record label. Each week we were to be paid a small retainer of £10 to pay the bills until we started gigging.

While things were starting to get off the ground with the new band I also did a Radio London Show and a photo session with my old mate Bernie Frost for his band Buster.

In February 1971 Bill and I did a little recording for a couple of days with the Stones mobile studio at Bill's house in Gedding. Bill had a few ideas he wanted to put down. It was fun being set up in the lounge and then we would go outside to listen to the tracks in the mobile studio.

Back home Roy and I started writing together and the partnership worked very well. It was agreed that we would write the numbers for the album and produce it ourselves. Mick had songs of his own plus we also wrote together as a band. Although Graham was a fine guitarist he had a problem at times getting the right sound, so we would suggest ideas.

Gilbert O'Sullivan had just hit big with a song called 'Nothing Rhymed' and he was booked into the studio on 3rd February to do a follow up. Gordon asked Mick and I if we would like to do the session. On arrival we met Gilbert, whose real name is Ray. There was just the one track with Gilbert on piano, Mick and myself. The song was called 'Underneath The Blanket Go' which had a few time signature changes. The session went well. Gilbert made us tea and chatted; he was very easy to get on with. I suggested over-dubbing hi-hats to give it a bigger sound which worked well. Gordon produced the single.

Gilbert O'SULLIVAN ○ *Distinctive Irish singer/songwriter/pianist. b. Raymond O'Sullivan, 1 December, 1946, Waterford. His unusual image – short trousers, flat cap and pudding-basin haircut – helped to launch the successful international career of the performer voted No 1 UK Male Singer of 1972*

145 wks

Date	Title	Pos	Wks
28 Nov 70 ●	NOTHING RHYMED *MAM 3*	8	11
3 Apr 71	UNDERNEATH THE BLANKET GO *MAM 13*	40	1
17 Apr 71	UNDERNEATH THE BLANKET GO (re-entry) *MAM 13*	42	3
24 Jul 71	WE WILL *MAM 30*	16	11
27 Nov 71 ●	NO MATTER HOW I TRY *MAM 53*	5	15
4 Mar 72 ●	ALONE AGAIN (NATURALLY) *MAM 66* ▲	3	12
17 Jun 72 ●	OOH-WAKKA-DOO-WAKKA-DAY *MAM 78*	8	11
21 Oct 72 ★	CLAIR *MAM 84*	1	14
17 Mar 73 ★	GET DOWN *MAM 96*	1	13
15 Sep 73	OOH BABY *MAM 107*	18	7
10 Nov 73 ●	WHY OH WHY OH WHY *MAM 111*	6	14
9 Feb 74	HAPPINESS IS ME AND YOU *MAM 114*	19	7
24 Aug 74	A WOMAN'S PLACE *MAM 122*	42	3
14 Dec 74	CHRISTMAS SONG *MAM 124*	12	6
14 Jun 75	I DON'T LOVE YOU BUT I THINK I LIKE YOU *MAM 130*	14	6
27 Sep 80	WHAT'S IN A KISS? *CBS 8929*	19	9
24 Feb 90	SO WHAT *Dover ROJ 3*	70	2

8 | Gilbert O'Sullivan | Underneath the Blanket Go | 1971 | *Holland 1 - Apr 1971 (10 weeks), Belgium 2 - Apr 1971 (10 weeks), UK 40 - Apr 1971 (4 weeks)*

It was strange seeing Gilbert on Top Of The Pops with a drummer miming to my playing. The track was not a big hit in the U.K. but entered the charts on 3rd April 1971 at Number 40 with a re-entry at 42 on the 17th for three weeks. It was however No.1 in the Netherlands and No. 2 in Belgium.

On one of my visits to Gordon's house which was on a private estate in Weybridge, he walked into the lounge carrying a baby tiger which we were able to stroke. He had his own small private zoo in the garden! Once when Goldie and I called in he asked if we were in a hurry to get home.   We ended up babysitting for him and his wife as they went out for the evening.   We were looking out for his little daughter Clair who was the little girl that Gilbert later wrote his big hit about.   She was a sweet little girl, no trouble at all.

We had all done various studio work in the past, with Mick and myself probably doing the most.   We recorded one track that I had co-written with Tucky Buzzard called 'Time Will Be Your Doctor', but it was with a different arrangement.   It featured Graham on guitar and turned out well.   Dave called in to the studio to have a listen which was nice.   Keith Harwood engineered the sessions.   I had worked with Keith on the Tucky Buzzard sessions.   He was one of the best.   Unfortunately at the age of 37 he died when his car left the road and crashed into a tree.   Ironically two weeks later on 16th September 1977 Marc Bolan was to meet his fate at the exact same spot.

Gordon popped by once and changed things on one track which we hated.   Once he had gone we redid it and used our version on the album.   Gordon did not really understand our type of music.   He was more familiar with Tom Jones and Englebert and to be fair he had tremendous success with them. All the album tracks were written, recorded and mixed by the end of April.

In May Bill asked me to do some sessions in France for John Walker of The Walker Brothers.   Bill was producing John doing a solo album.   Bill also suggested Graham on guitar.   It was agreed that we would rehearse at Bill's house in the South of France.

This was at the time of Mick Jagger's wedding to Bianca.   Bill had trouble getting a flight booked for Graham and myself, so in the end we were booked on the private plane on 12th May 1971 carrying wedding guests to the South of France.   Paul and Linda McCartney and family, Eric Clapton, Stephen Stills, Ringo and Maureen Starr, Ronnie Wood, Kenney Jones and Ian McLagan of The Faces were on board plus many other well-known people.   We were served a Champagne breakfast which was a pleasant surprise.

On arrival there were coaches and limousines waiting to take the guests to Mick and Bianca's Wedding Reception. Graham and I had a limo to ourselves. The Champagne had made us sleepy. I dozed off only to be woken by fans banging on the windows as we approached the Reception in St. Tropez.   At first I wondered what was going on; Graham was totally amazed by the whole thing.   This was all new for him.

Once inside we met up with Bill and enjoyed the Reception.   Terry Reid and his band were booked to play. Mick Jagger's father, Joe, came over and introduced himself.   The party was very enjoyable.   Steven Stills who looked a bit the worse for wear made his way to the stage and to my amazement he played OK. Terry's band played a good set. We met Mick and Bianca and the rest of the Stones.   In the early hours of the morning we made our way to Bill's villa where we were to stay.

The next day Mike Moran and John Walker arrived. Bill had some equipment at his house and said that I could arrange to get a kit once I arrived there.   Bill said to dial a number which was a music shop in Paris and just tell them what I needed saying that I was Charlie Watts and it would be billed to The Stones' office in London. I ordered a Ludwig kit and Zildjian cymbals; the same as my kit back home. Bill fancied having a kit so it would stay there after the sessions.   Two men drove from Paris to bring the kit to Bill's villa.   It is always nice to have a new instrument and I had a little time to get it set up and played in. Bill had a nice baby grand piano in the lounge and he would play piano as we went over the different arrangements; then we tried it as a band.

Whilst at Bill's I met Jim Gordon, the drummer who played on Joe Cocker's Mad Dogs and Englishmen LP and early Everly Brothers' tracks.   He co-wrote 'Layla' with Eric Clapton.   I also had the chance to jam with Carl Radle, Clapton's bass player.   Sadly Carl died some years later of alcoholism and Jim Gordon ended up in a mental hospital after killing his mother in a schizophrenic attack which was a shock as he seemed a really pleasant guy.

One day Keith Richards and his entourage (made up of family and friends) arrived. There was lots of laughter and drinking so no work got done for a few hours.   I had a long chat with Keith in the garden and found him to be a nice chap.

Poor Graham was not fitting in with everyone so it was decided by Bill to send him home and get another guitarist to join us.   He was an American called John Uribe who was in Europe at the time.   He told us that one day he was going to join The Stones. He was so sure of it, poor chap!

We spent a couple of weeks at Bill's rehearsing then moved on to Strawberry Studios at Chateau d'Heuroville near Paris.   We all went in Bill's car and the journey was good fun. The Chateau had the studio and accommodation, lovely gardens and a swimming pool.   Elton John had recorded an album there; it was a very well-known studio.   Bill invited Goldie to come over and Bill and I picked her up from the airport.   John's wife also arrived and Astrid was there with Bill.   We all ate together round a huge table in the dining room.   The girls looked after us during breaks from the recording.

The tracks went down well and sounded really good.   Bill is a good solid bass player to work with.   John was supposed to put down a few vocal tracks but due to a heavy consumption of alcohol was never quite up to it, so only guide vocals were used with

John to do them later once we had finished.   Bill also had the brass players who the Stones used put some tracks down.

Once the tracks were finished, Goldie and I flew home, leaving Bill to finish the mixing down.

Graham, unfortunately, was still not mixing that well with the rest of us; it was just different personalities. Finally it was agreed that he should be replaced. This did not go down very well with MAM as it was Graham who had been asked to put the band together in the first place. I never felt very comfortable about it but it was not working so we had no choice.

Garth Watt-Roy was the replacement guitarist. He had a good powerful voice which was a bonus. Gordon Mills was still looking at the rock market. We were back on track and started rehearsals. In June we had bought a second-hand van with a loan from MAM and had aircraft seats fitted in the back. We also bought some PA equipment.

111

Fuzzy Duck had been suggested as the band name and in July we had a promotional photo session on a duck farm in Aylesbury. Mick had a friend who would do the artwork for the album cover. It turned out brilliant. It was a duck with an Afro hair style with hippy clothes. It was very eye-catching. When the album was eventually released on 3rd September MAM had posters all over the advertising boards at the tube stations in London.

Garth had written a song called 'Double Time Woman' with heavy riffs very much in the mould of Deep Purple. We went into MAM studio on 22nd July and recorded it plus a track by Mick called 'Just Look Around You' for the B-side. Mike Cotton produced them. 'Double Time Woman' was released on 13th August. It was very commercial and Radio One played it a few times. I think with a bit more airplay it could have done well. We did a radio show for Ann Nightingale on 16th August. It was an In Session concert at the BBC for Sounds of The Seventies.

We started gigging at Universities and clubs. Our road manager was Barry Nash, known as Stirling, who fitted in well with our mad sense of humour. Roy was forever blowing his duck call which would have us in fits of laughter. It had featured on one of the tracks on the album. Roy had played with Arthur Brown before joining the Duck, and Mick with Andromeda.

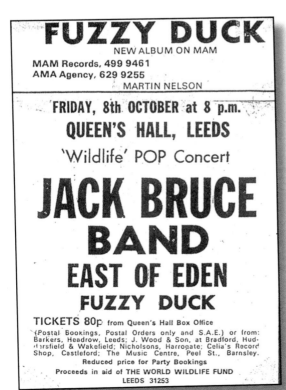

One of our first gigs was at The Marquee Club, Wardour Street, London on 23rd August 1971 and I got £4! We supported The Jack Bruce Band on 8th October at The Queens Hall, Leeds. My old mate Chris Spedding was playing for Jack so it was good to catch up with him again. East of Eden were also on the bill. The concert was in aid of The World Wildlife Fund.

The album was promoted but it failed to take off, however, 40 years later it became a collector's record! It was time for a new single for Fuzzy Duck. We went into the studio on 24th September. This time Gordon gave us a song which he wanted us to do. It was not really the type of number we would normally do in a heavy rock band. However, we gave it our best shot. It was called 'Big Brass Band' and had brass added

ALBUM ★ Reviews

Fuzzy Duck
Fuzzy Duck
★★★

Repertoire REPUK 1095
3,000-only reissue of classic acid blues-rock debut
This quartet, led by guitarist/vocalist Graham White, kicked off what would become their prog voyage with an eight-song mix of styles, bolstered here by four bonus cuts. Of these, the Double Dealing 45 sounds like a bass-heavy Deep Purple and Big Brass Band is a semi-acoustic, key-shifting slice of brass-rock a la Chicago. Better still is the straight-on rock of No Name Face, while album opener Time Will Be Your

88 Record Collector

Doctor is more typical syncopated blues-rock with fuzz guitar, chorale backing vocals and Daze Sharland's proggy organ tones. The intro to Mrs Prout cries out for sampling, reminiscent as it is of The Charlatans circa 1995, adopting a psych shuffle and percussion crescendo. More Than I Am also stands out with its sweet keys and tablas, before the Cream-esque Country Boy. A Word From Big D is period silliness, but investigating this further would be far from that. *Tim Jones*

on it. It was very much like a Blue Mink track and was quite commercial. Gordon was pleased with how quickly we got it put down and with the result. We recorded the B-side 'One More Hour' on 4th October. The single was released on 5th November which was also the date of our last gig at the French Institute in London.

'Big Brass Band' was to be our last recording. Garth was expecting more from MAM and I think Gordon was not really tuned in to the group and our style. The single had good reviews but failed to do anything. We decided to call it a day and go our separate ways. Goldie was working in London so we could pay the bills until I found something else.

● **FUZZY DUCK** (above), Islington's latest pop group to hit the big time, have just had their second single released, hot on the heels of their successful debut LP. The disc is "Big Brass Band" (MAM), a funky, punchy number, enhanced by a husky vocal.

Fuzzy Duck are the first British group to be signed up by pop world Svengali, Gordon Mills—the man who guided Tom Jones and Engelbert Humperdinck to the top. Said Paul Francis, the group's drummer, who hails from Liverpool Road: "Gordon has had fantastic success—he's not had a dud yet."

Gordon Mills has certainly proved to be the man with the golden touch in the pop world and, under his management, Fuzzy Duck should prosper.

During 1971 I did more sessions for various producers which I enjoyed. One was for Jimmy Justice who had a couple of hits in the early 60's with 'When My Little Girl Is Smiling' and 'Spanish Harlem'. The session was produced by Tony Ashton of Ashton Gardner and Dyke fame. Tony and I had previously had some good laughs at the Star-Club, Hamburg, so it was good to meet up again. I also played on a session for White Plains and that was strange having the band in the studio while we recorded the track.

After Fuzzy Duck split, I did some recording for Garth and we also did a few gigs under the name Garth.

Chapter 7

Tranquility

Early in 1972 my next band was a group called Tranquility. This band was signed to Epic an offshoot of CBS Records and had just had their first album released. The drummer had quit because he could not commit to the proposed touring. This band had already got America lined up which was fantastic for me as it was one country I wanted to visit.

Tranquility consisted of Bernard Hagley on bass, Terry Shaddick on guitar and vocals, Kevin McCarthy on guitar and vocals, Tony Lukyn on keyboards and vocals and Berkeley Wright on guitar and vocals. The album was called Tranquility and the band was managed by Ashley Kozak who had managed Donavon.

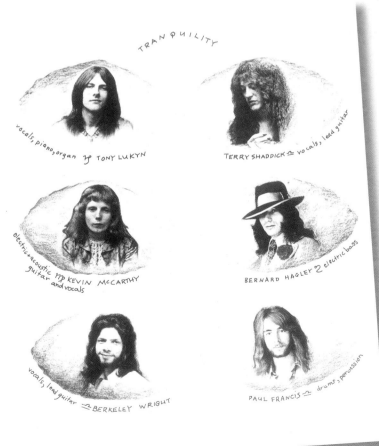

TRANQUILITY

vocals, piano, organ Tony LUKYN

TERRY SHADDICK — vocals, lead guitar

electric+acoustic guitar and vocals KEVIN McCARTHY

BERNARD HAGLEY — electric bass

vocals, lead guitar — BERKELEY WRIGHT

PAUL FRANCIS — drums, percussion

This band was totally different from Fuzzy Duck; beautiful vocals and melodic songs. The four part harmonies were outstanding. Terry was the main song writer and Tony also contributed songs. I was really pleased and excited about joining.

We had photos taken and although the album was already out in the UK the back photos would include me for the American market. The front cover illustration was lovely. It had a woman, her baby and two dogs sitting underneath a tree with rolling hills in the background. It also had a rainbow across the top with the name Tranquility. It was all very colourful and well done. The songs were very catchy.

We started rehearsing at Tony's house in Richmond. With six members it was a very full sound and all three guitarists had an individual style. Terry played more Rock style, Kevin Country and Berkeley more Jazz. It worked well. Each would take a solo depending on the style of the number. Bernie also did backing vocals and played flute and sax.

Ashley and his wife, Gypsy, had a vision for the band and wanted us to look the part visually as well as the music side. We found clothes that were individual and eye-catching for stage. In February we had two warm up gigs at the Rainbow Theatre, Finsbury Park opening for The Byrds.

Our first visit to the States was supposed to be a short visit of a couple of weeks to promote the album plus one or two gigs. It lasted ten weeks from 28th February until 9th May. A lot of travelling and not much money.

We flew to New York and stayed at a small hotel called The Gorham. The following day we flew to Los Angeles. We played three nights, 3rd, 4th and 5th March at the Fox West Theatre, Long Beach with Commander Cody and Linda Ronstadt. We then had five nights booked at The Whisky a Go Go in LA, a very well-known club. We supported Big Brother and The Holding Company. Janis Joplin used to sing with them. Her place was taken by Kathi McDonald. We also supported R.E.O. Speedwagon there at a later date. At the Academy of Music in New York on 22nd April we supported New Riders of the Purple Sage.

116

We often played at Universities which were good fun. We travelled in a large estate car which often took six band members plus Ashley and Gypsy. We had a driver and someone took a van with the equipment. Sometimes we took a short flight then hired an estate or station wagon as the Americans call them, and drove several hundred miles cramped in the back. But everything was so new; we were seeing things that we had only seen before on the television or cinema. It was all very exciting visiting new places and experiencing the different culture and seeing the various landscapes. On our second tour the colour of the trees during the autumn was amazing. Such long highways and vast open spaces. The Americans loved the English accent and were always very friendly.

I could not believe how well musicians were treated in America. In dressing rooms at the gigs we had dustbins full of ice with milk, beer and soft drinks and tables full of food. In England bands would be lucky to get a glass of water from the promoter. The other thing which was noticeable was the audience would listen no matter what type of music was played. If a country band followed a rock band there was no heckling from the crowd. Also unlike the UK, the audience would welcome the acts, and venues were full. Back home the venue would be half empty with people in the bar only appearing when the main act was on. Music is not pigeonholed in the States; if it is good it is appreciated. I would love every musician to have the chance to play there.

Most of the audiences were very appreciative of our music which meant so much to us. We had worked really hard to get it right. The boys' four part harmonies sounded so good. They would rehearse every day in the hotel with just a guitar. They had them off pat. Berkeley had the really high voice. It reminded me of Graham Nash in the Hollies, only Berkeley had a sound of his own.

I loved the fact that you could eat 24 hours a day. There were always places open. The pancakes and milk shakes were amazing. The only bad experience was when I had food poisoning from prawns at a Chinese Restaurant in China Town, New York. I was on my back for about 3 days. If I sat up I would be rushing to the bathroom to throw up. It was the worst feeling ever. It happened during a break from gigs which was really lucky.

The tour was due to finish at the end of May but we came home early because Ashley's house in England had been burgled. We were starting to get good reviews for the shows plus good press coverage on the album. I was pleased to return home and see Goldie again, but it felt empty gig-wise. We did one show in York and hated it. Crap dressing room, no drinks, nothing. It was usual for bands to be expected to change in the toilets.

On 31st July we started work on the new album at CBS, my old stomping ground with Tony Jackson. Keith Harwood had engineered their previous album but this time we had Mike Ross. I had previously worked on sessions with Mike, so it was good to see him again. We finished ten tracks. Terry wrote all but one which was written by Tony. Ashley produced the album.

We were excited about the recording; we had taken our time. Terry and Tony had come up with great songs. The album was to be called Silver. The artwork for the cover was a rainbow again with the band name and a photo of the band members on the back. The album came out in 1972 on Epic which was part of CBS.

It was soon time to return to America for another long tour; 27th October until 19th December. Most days we would travel 1,000 miles to gigs, often catching two internal flights then a drive. Again it was not easy at times with so many people packed into an estate car. First thing in the morning some people can be quite grumpy. I loved getting up early so had no problem waking up. We would have to leave the hotel very early most mornings in order to get to the next venue in time. Money was tight so we had to save wherever we could. We usually stayed at Holiday Inns. The twin rooms were big with two enormous beds. Either Tony or Bernie would share with me most of the time.

Many gigs were booked for us to support a well-known artist. This was great for us because it was a guaranteed large audience. We supported The Eagles, ZZ Top, David Bowie, Earth, Wind and Fire, Dr. Hook, Billy Preston, Yes, Mahavishnu Orchestra, Linda Ronstaat, Peter Frampton, New Riders of the Purple Sage, Captain Beefheart, R.E.O. Speedwagon, Dr. John, John Mayall, Edgar Winter, Bachman Turner Overdrive, and Black Oak Arkansas.

New York is renowned for Jazz Clubs. Elvin Jones, the drummer, was playing while we were there. I went on my own and stayed till the early hours of the morning watching two sets. I could not persuade the others to come. I think they were concerned about muggings, but I only dressed in jeans and a jean shirt and nobody took any notice. People walking around covered in gold are asking for trouble in certain areas. I do not wear a watch or jewellery. I caught a ring on a railing whilst running to catch a bus when I lived in Clapton. It tore a lump out of my finger and I was lucky not to lose the finger.

We had various people who worked for us as road crew. One chap had parked the van in Greenwich Village on 27th October after a gig. The back lock was cut through and all the equipment worth about $32,000 was stolen. We were gutted and to make matters worse we were due to support David Bowie in Pittsburg the following day. My insurance did not cover my equipment in America. It was in small print which my dad had not noticed.

Lucky for us CBS came to the rescue and advanced the money for us to finish the tour. We had to buy all new instruments then do the gig with David Bowie that night. It must have been terrible for the guys with new guitars. The Police said the equipment would have been out of the county within a few hours of it being stolen. I went to Manny's in New York, which was a great shop; you could get just about everything there. I just replaced my Ludwig kit and Zildjian cymbals. I had previously had half a kit stolen in England when working for Tony. Again that was someone breaking into the van. I learnt a lesson from these experiences and never leave any equipment in vehicles.

We picked up a lot of air plays and the venues were very well attended. The band was also getting odd radio shows to do. Terry was collecting fossils so we regularly had bags of rocks in the car. One night in a hotel Bernie had his trousers stolen from the bottom of his bed along with some money. It was just as well he never woke up; he may have been shot. It was a regular occurrence for three people to be murdered over a weekend in a small town. We were talking to a lawyer at one of our gigs and the conversation got round to hand guns, with that he produced a gun from a holster under his jacket. It took us all by surprise. He was very proud of it but it made us feel very uneasy.

There was a chocolate sweet called a Tootsie Roll; very tasty! They would often be left in the dressing room along with the drinks and people would give them as presents. Fans would often leave a joint on stage for the band. After a gig I found it helped to crash out and get a good night's sleep.

When it got close to our permit running out we would go over the border to Canada then we would be alright for a few more weeks. We played a gig at the Maple Leaf in Toronto with Dr. Hook and ZZ Top. My Aunt Dorothy and Uncle Tony lived in Toronto and I had the opportunity to meet up with them. I also spent some time with my cousin Christina and her husband Frank.

There were many flights across Amercia and on one flight when we were coming in to land at Kennedy Airport at night one of the band said to look at all the fire engines and ambulances down beside the runway. I said "Oh yeah!" but he was not joking.

I looked out the window and he was right. We landed on a special runway used for emergencies. Apparently there was a problem with the plane. When we had landed safely the pilot emerged from the cockpit looking dishevelled and the passengers burst into applause. Yoko Ono was on the flight and we sat talking to her while we were waiting to retrieve our musical equipment. It was major news that evening on the TV – Yoko Ono in plane scare!

On 9th November we played the Scope in Norfolk, Virginia; it was a big dome. It held eleven thousand people and we were supporting Yes. The show was sold out. Our dressing room was adjoining the dressing room for Yes and we had to walk through to get to the stage. Before the show during sound checks I saw Steve Howe putting on new strings. I reminded him of The Syndicats. He was not interested and it seemed to be an effort for him to talk. Stuff you, I thought. Success had obviously changed him or perhaps he had been caught on a bad day.

The manager of Yes told us we must only play for forty minutes, no more. Fine by us, we said. Our show went really well. They were a fantastic crowd that loved every minute. We came off as planned and walked back to our dressing room. The shouts and cheers were getting louder and louder from the audience. Then they started stamping their feet. Eleven thousand people doing that made quite a noise. Their manager came in our dressing room and said if you don't go back on the theatre management are frightened that they may start ripping the seats out!

It was a great feeling to hear such a big crowd wanting us back. We did our encore and as we came off stage Rick Wakeman from Yes said "Great show lads, well done." Not one of the others said a word, they just stood around looking as though they were sucking lemons, and they were another British band. They knew that they would do well because the crowd had come to seem them, not us. I will never forget that and was pleased that Rick still had his feet firmly on the ground. Good on you, Rick.

I enjoyed supporting The Eagles at Santa Barbara, L.A. on 3rd December. When we finished our set I stood side stage to watch their show. I had not realised how many songs Don Henley, the drummer, sang lead vocals on. He has such a distinctive voice. After a break of about fourteen years they started touring again.

The gig supporting the Everly Brothers was very special for me as I had grown up listening to their music from my brother's record collection. It is well known that they fell out for a while. On this gig they had separate dressing rooms. Phil was in our dressing room and Don in another. Phil was very friendly and loved the harmonies of our band. Coming from Phil Everly that was a fantastic compliment which really pleased everyone. I had seen so many pictures of them with their acoustic guitars and there he was. They sounded great but the backing band were average. They deserved better. They eventually split for many years then did a reunion concert in London in 1983 and they sounded as good as ever. They also had a fantastic band of session musicians behind them this time. I have always loved their harmonies. The Beatles were also very influenced by them.

It was interesting for us to be playing at small clubs one night then to a crowd of thousands the next, which was due to the main acts we were supporting.

Our last show on the second tour was at Carnegie Hall on 17th December 1972 supporting John Mayall. The only problem was we were in Springfield, Illinois and the whole airport was frozen over. The snow had really come down. This was a big gig for us and there was no way we were going to miss it.

Finally Ashley managed to charter two light aircraft to fly us to St. Louis then we would be able to get to New York from there. How on earth they managed to clear the runway and take off, I will never know. I slipped over twice just walking to the plane. I was thinking this is terrible, we must be mad trying to take off in a snow storm. I was trying to put the Buddy Holly incident out of my mind. I sat next to the pilot. Once we had cleared the snow and eventually started our ascent I started enjoying the flight. When we landed it felt like a bird landing with the wind tossing us about. We were all very relieved to be back on the ground.

Carnegie Hall was such a lovely building; it felt such an honour to play there and it was even better to read nice reviews the next day. It was one gig that we will all remember as a highlight of our tours.

Because Tranquility was spending so much time in America the possibility of moving there for a couple of years was discussed. This would have involved bringing our wives and partners. An option was Conneticut which was about an hour's drive from New York; very English looking with lots of green fields and open spaces. If the band had taken off big we would definitely have done that. After all, nothing was happening for us back home. In fact after one tour I was so short of money Terry got me a job for a month at a petrol station. It was in the evenings taking the money. I hated it but bills had to be paid and Goldie was doing her bit. I knew it was only until we went back to the States again.

Back in England Peter Frampton invited me over to his house. It was good to catch up on how things had been going. His wife, Mary, was there plus the model Twiggy. She was lovely and very friendly. Peter had bought one of the first video recorders. I had never seen one so Peter explained all about it. The ones nowadays are about a quarter of the size compared to when they first came out.

The third and final American tour for Tranquility started on 4th February and ended on 6th May 1973. We arrived in New York and needed to routine a few numbers and Ashley managed to get Atlantic Studios for four days for us to rehearse. The studio was huge and there was an old Sonor drum kit which had been set up by Bernard Purdie. This kit had been used on all the Atlantic sessions. It did not look great and it even had a hole from a cigarette burn in the floor tom. But it sounded great on records by Aretha Franklin and other Atlantic artists. It was great being in the studio; there was so much history. There was a tambourine which had tiny Zildjian cymbals for the jingles and it sounded fantastic. I have never seen one since.

TRANQUILITY consists of Terry Shaddick (vocals and guitar), Berkeley Wright (lead guitar), Tony Lukyn (keyboard), Bernard Hagley (bass guitar) and Paul Francis (drums).

Tranquility has recently released their second album "Silver" on Epic Records. This is their second engagement at the Capitol Theatre.

On 3rd March 1973 in Billboard's 'Bubbling Under the Top LP's' section the Tranquility LP was at No. 209.

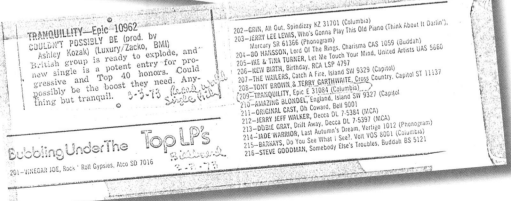

TRANQUILLITY—Epic 10962
COULDN'T POSSIBLY BE (prod. by Ashley Kozak) (Luxury/Zacko, BMI) British group is ready to explode, and new single is a potent entry for progressive and Top 40 honors. Could possibly be the boost they need. Anything but tranquil. 3-3-73

Bubbling Under The Top LP's

201—VINEGAR JOE, Rock 'n' Roll Gypsies, Atco SD 7016
202—GRIN, All Out, Spindizzy KZ 31701 (Columbia)
203—JERRY LEE LEWIS, Who's Gonna Play This Old Piano (Think About It Darlin'), Mercury SR 61366 (Phonogram)
204—BO HANSSON, Lord Of The Rings, Charisma CAS 1059 (Buddah)
205—IKE & TINA TURNER, Let Me Touch Your Mind, United Artists UAS 5660
206—NEW BIRTH, Birthday, RCA LSP 4797
207—THE WAILERS, Catch A Fire, Island SW 9329 (Capitol)
208—TONY BROWN & TERRY GARTHWAITE, Cross Country, Capitol ST 11137
209—TRANQUILITY, Epic E 31084 (Columbia)
210—AMAZING BLONDEL, England, Island SW 9327 (Capitol
211—ORIGINAL CAST, Oh Coward, Bell 9001
212—JERRY JEFF WALKER, Decca DL 7-5384 (MCA)
213—DOBIE GRAY, Drift Away, Decca DL 7-5397 (MCA)
214—JADE WARRIOR, Last Autumn's Dream, Vertigo 1012 (Phonogram)
215—BARKAYS, Do You See What I See?, Volt VOS 8001 (Columbia)
216—STEVE GOODMAN, Somebody Else's Troubles, Buddah BS 5121

We enjoyed supporting the other acts but it was around Carolina that we did very well on our own. On 13th March we played at The University of North Carolina in Wilmington. Jo Jo Gunne who had a big hit in America were on with us as were Gentle Giant. The promoter wanted Gentle Giant to open the show followed by Jo Jo Gunne with Tranquility to close the show. Jo Jo were not happy because the promoter said we were more popular in the area. It was very awkward for us so in the end we let Jo Jo close the show. Gentle Giant also had a good following in England.

We loved Carolina and made some good friends there. One of my favourite pastimes was walking along the beach and looking for small sharks' teeth which were

washed up by the tides. On one of our visits to Carolina we went on the beach and Terry and Kevin got badly sunburnt and had to do a gig that evening feeling really awful.

When we returned there seven weeks later someone who was connected with booking the band told me our money had gone up a lot since the first gig. At the time we were living on about five to ten dollars a day each. Food would be laid on at the venues so we did not have to buy food most of the time. It was not cheap to keep a six piece band on the road. But this remark set off alarm bells. The fee had gone from seven hundred dollars to over two thousand dollars.

On the second visit to Wilmington the whole band was invited to dinner with Terry and Jane Moore who had become fans of the band. It was great to eat a decent meal as most of the food on the road is pretty bad at times. I am pleased to say they still keep in touch. Terry is a great artist.

When we opened for the Mahavishnu Orchestra, Billy Cobham was on drums, and to my amazement during a section without drums he was doing press-ups behind the drum kit!

MELODY MAKER, May 19, 1973—

TRANQUILITY

FOR the second week in a row, New York's Academy of Music presented an English band who had been hard at work touring the States, but is virtually unknown at home.

Last week it was Foghat who got a tumultuous reception at Howard Stein's theatre and this week Tranquility who opened the show for Peter Frampton and J. Geils.

The search for something sparkling fresh in music should stop at Tranquility. Unlike any other band I've seen, they combine the California flair for four part vocal harmonies with the zesty energy of English rock.

Lead singer and guitarist Terry Shaddick, resplendent in a glittering silver sequined coat, comes across as engaging a personality as Rod Stewart, communicating that same sense of having a wonderful time on stage.

In addition to Shaddick, Tranquility includes Tony Lukyn, keyboards and vocals; Berkeley Wright, lead guitar and vocals; Kevin McCarthy, rhythm guitar and vocals; Bernard Hagley, bass guitar and flute; Paul Francis, drums and percussion. After their Academy date, the band returned to England to begin work on a third album and their schedule plans for a European tour.

For the benefit of Jagger watchers, Mick turned up at the Academy on the second night of this bill and reportedly wanted to join Frampton for "Jumpin' Jack Flash" but couldn't because it could have caused security problems. — LORAINE ALTERMAN.

TRANQUILITY, "EAGLE EYE" (prod. by Ashley Kozak) (Luxury/Zacko, BMI). There's nothing tranquil about this thumper from the highly acclaimed English contingent. Strong vocals support a melody that continually rises in excitement. Should literally fly up the charts. Epic 10941.

We also supported Joe Walsh and his band Barnstorm, Dr. Hook and The Medicine Show, Bob Seger and J. Geils Band. We did several dates with Peter Frampton. With America being such a large country some artists would be big in some states but not so much in others. Peter was getting a good name for himself; with John Siomos on drums, Rick Wills on bass and Andy Bown they were a tight band. Peter would suffer from nerves and would often have to be called from the toilet to start his set. He went on to big success in America with a massive selling live album Frampton Comes Alive. I got on well with John and he visited Goldie and me in London. Sadly he died in 2004. He was a great drummer who had played on many hit records.

By the end of the third tour we were told that there would be no money to take home as the tour had gone into the red due to the bills for hotels and travelling. I went to see Howard Stein who was in charge of finance and also owner of the Academy Theatre in New York. I explained that I had a wife and bills to pay back in England. The result was I was paid. To go home with nothing after over three months away would have been terrible. We are only talking about 600 dollars spread over three months, it is very small.

At some point during the tours I got to meet up with the boys in Tucky Buzzard and watched them play Madison Square Gardens. I also saw them at a couple of other gigs. Bill was at one and he introduced me to John Lee Hooker.

On one occasion Ashley told me I was needed back in New York for a session. I knew we were all going in a few days but my reaction was who knows me in America to do a session. Ashley said I could fly back with Corrie our road manager and they would join me the next day. I didn't need to take my kit as there would be one there.

Corrie dropped me off at the location, only it did not look much like a studio. As I entered I realised it was a restaurant and a very nice one at that. I was ushered to a large table and who should be sitting there grinning at me was one Bill Wyman. The whole thing was a surprise for me. The rest of the band had been in on the secret. Bill had bumped into Ashley and found out I was in the States and fixed the surprise. It was really good to see him. As I took my seat along with the other friends of Bill I heard a very distinctive voice coming from the table behind me. It can't be, I thought. I had to take a quick look. I turned round and saw that Orson Wells, the actor, was sitting right behind me. We had a lovely meal.

Coming back from a tour it always took a few days to adjust to a completely different way of life from being on the road. It is a strange feeling as you are relieved to get away from everyone but you miss it once you are home for a while. You get restless to play again. If we had had work to come home to that would have helped. The first week was usually spent catching up on lost sleep. The tours had been very long; ten weeks, two months and three months. I used to get so excited about coming home I would stay up the night before we flew back thinking I would sleep through the flight, but it never worked so I would arrive home shattered having been awake for two nights.

I could not see a great future for me with the band because of the management. I liked Ashley but it was obvious he was always going to be in control of the band. The band never had much say in things. By this time Berkeley was planning to leave. We cut our final album in England. A different bass player was brought in, which was wrong. There was a lot of unrest within the band. I decided to leave and Berkeley and I left at the same time. It was such a shame as the band was so good and had so much to offer.

Terry, Kevin and Tony stayed out in America. Terry co-wrote Physical for Olivia Newton-John which was a big hit in 1981. Tony and Kevin continued writing and one of Kevin's songs featured on the Hollies' 2009 album Then, Now, Always.

Chapter 8

Maggie Bell

I started doing more sessions and was offered a residency at a restaurant called The Stable in Cromwell Road. Nick Newell was on sax and flute and Eric Leese played keyboards. We started at 10 p.m. and finished at two in the morning. I left to go to work as Goldie was getting ready to go to bed. Quite a few well-known actors visited the restaurant. I left my old Trixon kit there set up all the time. For most of the night I would use brushes or one stick and one brush. The tables were very close to the stage area with a small dance floor so the volume had to be low. This was good as I could work on my technique at playing soft. We played standards to more current material. Eric and Nick were good players. Nick later went on to work with The Kinks.

It was while doing a session in early 1974 that I met the guitarist Hughie Burns. There were a lot of musicians on the session. Tristan Fry played percussion and Albert Lee was on guitar. Hughie asked me if I was interested in doing some work with Maggie Bell. Maggie had just left the band Stone The Crows to go solo and later on was to be voted Best Female Singer four years in a row. Hughie then mentioned the dreaded American tour lined up.

MAGGIE TOURS IN MAY—official

MAGGIE BELL has now finalised her new support group, who will back her on her upcoming concert tours of both America and Britain. She is now confirmed to open her debut U.S. solo tour at the Santa Monica Civic Stadium in Los Angeles on March 3, and she then goes on to play a five-week coast-to-coast itinerary. A spokesman said this week that Maggie will definitely undertake a major British tour during May, and that dates and venues will be announced shortly.

Line-up of Maggie's backing band is Paul Francis (drums), Hugh Burns (guitar), Mike Moran (keyboards), Smiley Jones (percussion) and Pat Donaldson (bass) with the Thunder Thighs on back-up vocals. Most of the musicians are top session men, though Donaldson was formerly with Sandy Denny's Fotheringay.

It is now confirmed that Maggie's debut album "Queen Of The Night" will be issued by Polydor on February 15. And within the next week or two, the label plans to rush out a single extracted from the album — Maggie's version of the Ringo Starr song "Oh My My".

Among musicians featured on the LP — which was produced by Jerry Wexler — are Cornell Dupree (guitar), Richard Tee (keyboards), Steve Gadd (drums), Chuck Rainey (bass) and Bill Salter (also bass). Vocal backings are by the Sweet Inspirations.

I thanked him but said no as I had just finished three very long tours over there and wanted to spend more time at home.

On returning home I mentioned it to Goldie who said that not every situation was the same and this one could be more beneficial and I should at least find out about it. I thought about it and called Hughie the next day saying I was interested. He had also spoken to another drummer but would prefer me to do it. We agreed to meet up with the other musicians involved. Mike Moran was on keyboards, Pat Donaldson on bass and a lady group of backing singers called Thunder Thighs. What a great name!

Maggie had just released her first solo album entitled Queen of the Night which had been recorded in the States with Steve Gadd on drums, Cornell Dupree on guitar and Chuck Rainey on bass. It was produced by Jerry Wexler who had also produced Aretha Franklin's albums. Steve is a great drummer who I had the pleasure of meeting in 2010.

We met at Maggie's management office in February. Mark London was her manager along with Peter Grant who was managing Led Zeppelin. Mark was a fun guy. He spoke really fast and reminded me a little of Groucho Marx. Maggie was great, really down to earth. We were given copies of the tracks from Queen of the Night to learn.

The rehearsal went well. Pat was a solid bass player to work with. Hughie and Mike were also gifted players. Thunder Thighs were the three backing girl singers who sounded good and we all got on well during rehearsals. The tour started on 3rd March

1974 at the Santa Monica Civic Stadium L.A. with Peter Frampton's Camel and Poco. We had dates on our own plus other dates with Peter Frampton's new band Frampton's Camel and an English band called Foghat who were building up a good reputation in America.

Maggie has an amazing voice. She can sing any style. I have never worked with any female singer since who has come anywhere near Maggie vocal-wise. The shows went well and as we got into our stride the band got tighter. Maggie was all over the stage, a great performer. She commanded attention and got it. The reviews were very good.

I felt a lot happier with this set up. The wages were very good and all hotels would be paid. The money was paid every week but most of the time I did not want to carry it around with me so I just took some pocket money and would get the balance at the end of the tour. I trusted Maggie 100% so I had no worries there.

During the tour Mike had his drink spiked, most probably with LSD. Poor Mike he was in a terrible state. The girls from Thunder Thighs sat up during the night with him just talking and telling him he would be OK. It lasted into the next day. It must have been awful for him not knowing what was happening to his body. After that I would never pick up a drink if I had left it. It was a game some people played to spike drinks for a laugh. It is a really silly and dangerous thing to do.

At one gig in the Deep South whilst supporting Earth, Wind & Fire, Maggie sat behind a screen on stage for the opening number of the set. When she came forward from behind the screen the audience were really surprised to see that a white woman from Scotland could sing the blues. The response was amazing.

The tour went well and we returned back to the U.K. for a few weeks before the second tour. Maggie received good reviews for her first solo album. I was so pleased for her. She had been through a bad time with Stone The Crows when her boyfriend the guitarist Les Harvey was electrocuted on stage and died.

On our return to England we learned that Maggie had been added to a Who show at Charlton Football Ground on 18th May 1974. Dave Mason had cancelled and Maggie was the replacement. This was a huge show and was on all day with various other supporting acts including Humble Pie, Bad Company, Lou Reed, and Lindisfarne. Lulu who was a fellow Scot and old friend of Maggie came to our dressing room and had a chat. She was charming. Roger Daltry also stopped by to say hello. I did not get the chance to see many of the acts as they had been on before we arrived. Maggie was on just before The Who.

It was reported afterwards that the venue was excellent but the event had been spoilt by greed of the organisers who seemed intent on squeezing more and more people into the ground which was already bursting at the seams with an extra five to ten thousand people who should not have been there.

When I looked out at the size of the audience it blew me away. They say there were 74,000 people there. It was just a mass of people as far as the eye could see plus people were standing on balconies in the blocks of flats overlooking the ground. It was an amazing sight.

Below: Lindisfarne on stage, view from the stage at Charlton Football club

I was on a very large drum rostrum on the stage. I really enjoyed the gig but we did have a few gremlins. Hughie's guitar amp went off during the first number and that left a big hole in the sound. It seemed to take ages to come back on. Maggie cut her hand on her tambourine, but we soldiered on. We had some good reviews and a few saying the problems spoilt the show.

The Who played at 70,000 watts and the show was put in the Guinness Book of Records as the loudest concert. The whole event was an amazing experience for us.

The second American tour kicked off. This time we also played at clubs along with the bigger venues including the Schaefer open air concert on 17th June in Central Park, New York. We opened a new club in Chicago. As well as doing gigs on our own, we supported the Doobie Brothers on a few shows. The Doobie Brothers were laid back and it was fun working with them.

We also supported Blue Oyster Cult and Lynyrd Skynyrd.   We supported Procol Harum on six dates. One was in Washington at the Kennedy Centre which was a really lovely building by the river. Maggie would often steal the headlines the next day in the papers. Procol Harum were good musicians but so boring to watch. Their drummer B. J. Wilson was good and I enjoyed his playing. They had a grand piano supplied for the tour which we were also meant to use but they made us hire another one saying that we were putting it out of tune.   Mike had been classically trained. Two grand pianos on stage at a gig; it was a joke.

Bette Midler turned up at one venue and spent a long time back stage with us. She was super and great fun to be around.   Her musicians must really have a ball working for her. On another occasion Grace Slick of Jefferson Airplane came back stage for a chat. It was not unusual for various artists to come backstage to chat to Maggie and the band. Rod Stewart and Elton John arrived together at one gig.

The one date on this tour I had been looking forward to was Madison Square Gardens, New York when we were to support The Who. Having seen Tucky Buzzard play there I was hoping that I would one day have the chance to play there.   At last I had got there.   Having previously played at Carnegie Hall, this was the next most prestigious venue to play.

The gig on 10th June 1974 at Madison Square Gardens was amazing.   The place was really buzzing that night. We never saw The Who backstage, someone said they had a row in the dressing room, but that may just be hearsay. We went out front to listen to them.   The sound was bad from where we were standing in a tiered section. I would think on ground level it was better.

Playing at Madison was fantastic.   It was packed; about twenty thousand people or more.   Looking up at the tiers of seats there were thousands of lit cigarette lighters. It was an amazing sight.   I felt quite lost on such a huge stage.   It was like a giant cake with candles. The gig went well and it was a real thrill to finally play there.

On one of Maggie's gigs supporting Uriah Heep, we had Bill Wyman, half of Zeppelin and Bad Company, and Roy Harper watching.   I had to smile thinking if only the audience knew who was backstage.

On another occasion we had been invited to meet with Gary Glitter who was over in the States. I was with John Bonham and as we walked into the building he said it was embarrassing. I enquired why and he said he had been asked by his son, Jason, to get Gary's autograph.   I said I didn't think he would mind but John felt uncomfortable about asking.

On leaving there was a party to go to. Maggie, me and big Brian, who looked after us, got into Gary's limo. He said there was plenty of room so Paul Rogers got in behind us plus a couple of members of The Average White Band. Gary sat in the front. Suddenly an argument started between Paul and one of the Average White Band. A window opened and a pair of glasses belonging to the chap from The Average White Band were thrown out. Gary was calling for calm from the front seat. The limo stopped and the glasses were retrieved. The whole episode was surreal.

The record label Swan Song had been launched by Peter Grant and Led Zeppelin. Various launch parties were held and we attended one. I remember feeling a little fragile the next day due to the champagne flowing the previous night. It was always good to meet up with Zeppelin. Life was never dull that's for sure. It was at one of their parties that I witnessed a television switched on full blast with a long lead going out of a window and crashing to the ground several floors below. One of the members of the band disappeared into a bedroom, the next minute a pair of knickers came out of the door; these were filled with ice cubes and ceremoniously tossed out of the window. There was no shortage of anything at the party and it was my one and only experience of cocaine. It did nothing for me and I never tried it again.

During the tour we played one night in Las Vegas. Walking from the aircraft into the airport building there were slot machines everywhere you looked, even in the toilets. The show went well and we spent a little time watching the gaming tables. I had a go and lost about 20 dollars in a few minutes so decided I would stop at that. There were people sitting at the tables with piles of hundred dollar bills amounting to thousands of dollars. I had been all over America with Tranquility but had never been to Vegas before, so I enjoyed the experience.

One venue in San Francisco seemed to have had all the air sucked out of it and as the door leading onto the stage was opened the heat was overwhelming. The place was packed to the rafters. It was like walking into a furnace and I found it very difficult to breathe during our performance. I have never experienced anything like that since.

On returning home I started to get sessions with Mike, Hughie and Pat. We worked well together. We called ourselves The National Debt band doing sessions for the Marsha Hunt Show on Capital Radio. We backed H. B. Barnham who had worked with Michael Jackson for a show in London and we had brass on that one. I also got to do a couple of sessions with Herbie Flowers the bass player. Herbie later joined Sky with John Williams and Tristan Fry.

Back home it was time for Maggie to start a follow up album to Queen of the Night and Mark London was to produce this one. We started running through the new material; we had songs by Zoot Money, Colin Allen who was Maggie's drummer from Stone The Crows, Leo Sayer, Pete Wingfield, Simon Kirke and Paul Kossoff, Lennon and McCartney, Phil May from the Pretty Things plus a version of Wishing Well by Free. All good numbers.

Ringo Starr had bought Tittenhurst Park in Ascot from John Lennon. There was a studio in the house called Startling Studios. Maggie booked it during September for the recording. There were two cottages in the grounds where we could stay. The house and grounds with acres of land were fantastic. Ringo and his wife Maureen were there. We had use of the swimming pool and mini motor bikes to roar around the grounds which were good fun.

The room where we set up was the large white lounge which featured in John Lennon's video of him playing piano and singing 'Imagine'. The control room area was looking down on to the lounge close to the kitchen. The fridge in the kitchen was full all the time with lagers and beers for us to help ourselves. The whole atmosphere was ideal for recording. We went in to record when we felt like it which was nearly always evening time. Goldie came down and stayed one weekend.

Maggie wanted to do a version of The Beatles' "I Saw Her Standing There" changing the "her" to "him". We had been doing this number on tour which always got a good response and Maggie sang it so well. Maggie would often put her vocals down with a track as a rough guideline for the band, but on this track she wanted to keep the vocal track and have the song sounding as live as possible. The number was put down and we went back to the control room to find Ringo and Paul McCartney sitting there listening. They seemed to enjoy the version. It was strange doing one of Paul's songs with him there.

On another day we had put down a slow track where I played very laid back tom fills. When I went into the control room Ringo was sitting there. I said he probably thought I had ripped off one of his fills as it was in his style. He replied "No, fuck it. I ripped it off somebody else anyway!" to which we both laughed.

I sat down with him one day and we talked about drums for about twenty minutes. He told me how he would take ages getting the old calf skin heads tuned up only to have someone open a studio door and let cold air in and they would have to be tuned again. He was saying how much easier it was with the new plastic heads. You would think he may be bored talking drums but far from it.

After doing one track, which was probably Suicide Sal, we were talking about tap dancing when Ringo said he did a bit and it was agreed that he would do some on the track. He disappeared to find his tap shoes and that was the last we saw of him until the next morning. He was funny. Maureen was very nice; she would often pop in to have a listen.

134

Terry Taylor from Tucky Buzzard played on two tracks along with Hughie and a guitarist called Brian Breeze who was joining the band as Hughie had other commitments. Jim Jewell from my old band Pepper played sax on one track. There were even bagpipes put on. Jimmy Page played on two tracks but his part was put down after we had finished recording. There were also two other guitarists who put bits down. Delisle Harper was brought in on bass and Pete Wingfield on keyboards. Roy Davis also did some keyboard work and Simon Kirke played keyboards on his number. Martin Rushent engineered the sessions.

One day John Bonham arrived at the studio. I had seen the rock star party side of John and it was strange to see him turn up in a Range Rover wearing a flat cap looking every bit the Country Squire. Maggie asked him if he would like to do a track. He looked a little unsure so I said he could use my kit. John also played Ludwig drums. I walked over to the drum booth with him and we checked a few things and I walked back to the control room as he started to play. The power was amazing. John had a sound of his own. No matter what kit he sat behind it would still sound like John Bonham. For me he was the best rock drummer I had heard. He had great technique along with the power. For some reason the track with John playing was not used on the album.

The gardens were lovely and there were large models of dinosaurs and some had little soldiers climbing ropes up them. These were things that Lennon had done before Ringo moved in. There was a lovely old gypsy caravan by a lake, which I am told belonged to his son Julian.

I have always loved Punch and Judy and one day Ringo hired one for his son's birthday party. It went down very well, grown ups included! Paul McCartney arrived with his family. I had met him several times before; at Olympic Studios and Mick Jagger's wedding reception and found him to be a very easy-going person.

It was great to play with Jim Jewell again. He had just done sessions for Al Stewart and Joan Armatrading. He played a great solo on a blues track by Phil May called 'It's Been So Long'. Looking back at the recording of Suicide Sal it brings back great memories. We were there for a couple of weeks. The album was finished but it was not released until the following year, 1975.

Goldie and I wanted to have our own house but could not afford to buy in London. The house next door was on the market for £14,000. We did not have anyway near that sort of money, if we had we may have made an offer. However it would be good to get away from the traffic and we had also been robbed twice which was not very pleasant. The first time was when I lived there before we were married. All my jackets were taken and they had used letters which they set fire to so they could see where they were going. They returned the following day and stole a length of rolled up new carpet.

The second time was when we were both living there. I had just finished recording sessions with Tranquility. Goldie had the day off work and I had just picked up a tape of the new songs. We decided to go to Epping Forest for a walk and then hear the tape later. On our return we discovered the burglary. Half the stereo had gone along with various other items including jewellery and leather jackets. They must have been disturbed or got windy as they left the speakers on the floor ready to be disconnected. The tape machine had been taken with the tape inside it. I was really gutted. That hurt more than anything else. They also stole two antique ornaments that had belonged to Goldie's family which really upset her.

We found a semi-detached house in Silver End near Witham in Essex. It was not too far for either of us to commute to work in London. I converted the back of the garage into a small studio so I could do some teaching.

Maggie and the band did an eight date UK tour in the autumn with The Pretty Things. The line up was Pete Wingfield on keyboards, Mo Foster on bass and Brian Breeze on guitar. We rehearsed at Manticore rehearsal rooms which were a converted old cinema in Fulham owned by Emerson Lake and Palmer.

RAINBOW THEATRE
FINSBURY PARK General Manager : D. J. COUNTER

JOHN SMITH ENTERTAINMENTS presents

MAGGIE BELL in Concert

Special Guests THE PRETTY THINGS

THURSDAY, OCTOBER 3rd, 1974

EVENING 7-30

STALLS
£1·65
Incl. VAT

F45

FOR CONDITIONS OF SA

TO BE RETAINED

Left:
Brian,
Mo, Paul,
Maggie, Pete

136

We opened at The Apollo in Glasgow on 27th September, Maggie's home town. Peter Grant held a small party in his hotel suite and Jimmy Page called in. Robert Plant and John Bonham gave their support to our gig at The Town Hall, Birmingham on 2nd October. I remember John telling me a great story about when he went to see a band play; it may have been East of Eden. He got talking to the drummer who asked if he played drums and John said he did. The chap asked what was the name of John's band. When John replied Led Zeppelin the poor guy nearly fell on the floor with shock.

On 3rd October 1974 we had a great gig at the Rainbow Theatre, Finsbury Park with the Pretty Things as special guests. Pete Wingfield was superb with his white tails. Mo Foster actually recorded the gig and released a live album in 2002.

One night on arriving back at the hotel after a gig we asked the night porter if we could get something to eat. We went to the kitchen with him. He opened the fridge and said he could do ham sandwiches. One of the band spotted a whole cooked chicken in there. When the chap went off to make the sandwiches the chicken was removed and devoured. The carcass was left outside Phil May's bedroom door. As we walked past in the morning, Phil was standing in the doorway half asleep with the manager accusing him of nicking the chicken and Phil saying he knew nothing about it.

Life on the tour bus was hilarious, with Mark London doing his cabaret act and guitarist Brian Breeze pacing up and down the bus impersonating an eccentric Welsh lay preacher.

We also did a gig at The Rainbow Theatre with the Dutch group Focus. It was for a foreign TV show and we played for about 20 minutes.

CENSORED!

I had lots of sessions the beginning of 1975 including ones for Carl Wayne of the Move, Marion Montgomery and Geno Washington. I also did an LP for Brian Friel called Arrivederci Ardrossan which was also released in the USA as Ashes to Matchsticks. On 14th February I backed Marsha Hunt at Dingwalls in Camden Town, for which I was paid £25. I was also doing some teaching in my converted garage studio.

It was time for Maggie to promote her new album 'Suicide Sal' in Europe. We opened in Oslo on 3rd March, followed by Copenhagen 4th March, Hamburg 7th March, Frankfurt 8th March, Zurich 9th March, Brussels 10th and 11th March, finishing in Paris on 12th March. Hudson Ford was the support act.

On Maggie's third American tour we were to support Bad Company who had taken off big in the States. The tour was for five weeks and started on 7th May 1975 at the Sportatorium, Miami Beach, Florida.

Most of the venues were very large and would vary from 10,000 to 20,000 people. This was an ideal tour for Maggie and it would be a good opportunity to play tracks from the new album. It would also give us another chance to play Madison Square Gardens again.

The tour soon got into its stride. Big Brian was always great fun. Brian was Welsh and always got on with everyone. Before he died he had the chance to work with Led Zeppelin for a while. When Brian and Peter Grant stood next to each other nothing got past them. They were big guys. I think Peter Grant was the best manager I had come across. He would do anything for his boys in Zeppelin. I really liked the man. Most of his work was done on a hand shake, not tying the band up for years on a dodgy contract. The days of promoters ripping bands off were over with Peter. The promoter would get a small percentage and the band took the rest. 10% of a fifty thousand seat stadium sold out in hours was not worth turning down for more. All the merchandise was also strictly controlled.

After one show Maggie and I were the last to leave the theatre. Big Brian had gone to get the car and we waited outside the stage door. Later back at the hotel we found out that one person had been stabbed to death and the Police had shot and killed the attacker right where we had been standing. On another occasion a sniper on the theatre roof was taking shots at the audience leaving the building. It's a strange old world. You just had to get on with things otherwise you would be forever looking over your shoulder.

Our date at Madison Square Gardens was halfway through the tour on 30th May 1975. We were staying at the New York Sheraton Hotel. Coming down in the lift one morning

BAD COMPANY TOUR 1975

SPECIAL GUEST STAR MAGGIE BELL

Date.	Location
May 7	Sportatorium, Miami Beach, Fla.
9	Civic Center, Lakeland, Fla.
12	Municipal Auditorium, Atlanta, Georgia.
14	Coliseum, Greensboro, N.Carolina.
15	Hampton Roads Coliseum, Virginia.
16	Civic Center, Charleston.
18	Hara Arena, Dayton, Ohio.
19	Stadium, Chicago, Illinois.
21	Arena, Toledo, Ohio.
22	Municipal Auditorium, Cleveland, Ohio.
25	Coliseum, New Haven, Connecticut.
26	Spectrum, Philadelphia, PA.
27	Civic Auditorium, Baltimore, Maryland.
28	Civic Center, Pittsburgh, PA.
30	Madison Square Garden, New York.
31 – June 1	Music Hall, Boston, Mass.
2	Civic Center, Niagara Falls, New York.
4	Olympia Stadium, Detroit, Michigan.
6	Convention Center, Indianapolis, Ind.
7	Kiel Auditorium, St. Louis, Missouri.
8	Tulsa Assembly Center, Oklahoma.
10	Coliseum, Houston, Texas.
11	Arena, San Antonio, Texas.
12	Memorial Auditorium, Dallas, Texas.
13	Memorial Auditorium, Kansas City, Missouri.
15	Coliseum, Denver, Colorado.
17	Arena, Seattle, Washington.
19	Winterland, San Francisco, Calif.
20	Auditorium, Sacramento, Calif.
21	Forum, Los Angeles, Calif.
22	Sports Center, San Diego, Calif.

there were Paul Rogers, Simon Kirk, myself and a few other people plus Joe Bugner the British Heavyweight Champion boxer. Bugner was due to fight Muhammad Ali on 30th June in Kuala Lumpar, Malaysia with the fight being shown live on a big screen at Madison Square Gardens. We had a chat with him and wished him luck. He would need it facing Muhammad Ali.

Bad Company was a great band and Simon is a really solid drummer, never over playing. His style with Boz on bass worked really well. Paul Rogers has a fabulous voice. 'Alright Now' by Free and 'Can't Get Enough of Your Love' by Bad Company are classic tracks. 'Feel Like Making Love' was another great live number. I enjoyed watching them play from the wings. The guys were fine to get on with. Paul would get himself into a few problems with people at times but I always found him pleasant.

Bad Company had their own plane chartered for the tour. Peter Grant was about quite a lot plus Richard Cole who looked after Led Zeppelin on the road. Peter would not stand any nonsense from anybody giving his acts grief. He would always make sure everything was OK for us all. Richard was the same. They had both worked at the highest level with Led Zeppelin so everything ran fine when they were around.

The show at Madison went well. Then we made our way to Boston for the next date. Delisle Harper was on bass. He was a really good bass player to work with and always had a smile on his face. Lynton Naiff was on keyboards, Geoff Whitehorn on guitar along with Joe Jammer from Chicago. Geoff and I roomed together most of the time. Shaven headed Joe would cook up brown rice and Tuna fish in his room which he ate all the time. I must admit it tasted good when you were hungry. Once we told him he could get mercury poisoning from the Tuna and he cut down a bit.

94 CHICAGO SUN-TIMES, Wed., May 21, 1975

Chicagoan Joe Jammer, performing with Maggie Bell in the Stadium Monday, decided to shave for the concert. (Sun-Times Photo by Larry Graff)

Joe Jammer, guitar; Geoff Whitehorn, guitar; Paul Francis, drums; Delisle Harper, bass; Lynton Naiff, keyboards. Chicago Stadium, Monday.

MAGGIE BELL: Maggie Bell, vocals; There weren't any goofs in Maggie Bell's opening set. She and her new band nearly stole the show with a combination of tight, rocking instrumentals and Maggie's beautiful voice. She could sing a haunting folk-style "I Was in Chains" (which featured some nice echo on the a cappella ending), rock mightily on "What You Got," "If You Don't Know" and "I Saw Him Standing There" (a reworking of the Beatles classic that is now a Bell classic) and get down to the blues dirt on "Penicillin Blues" and the encore of "Going Down." Her two guitarists, billiard-shaven Joe Jammer (who as Joe Wright grew up in Chicago) and Geoff Whitehorn, played some stunning solos.

Reprinted from yesterday's late editions.

140

Geoff and Joe would take extended solos which the crowds loved. They are both fine players. Sometimes we would leave Geoff on stage playing while we all went off for about ten minutes. Geoff actually went on to play for Bad Company some years later.

The tour had taken us to Atlanta, Charleston, Chicago, Philadelphia, Detroit, Pittsburgh, Oklahoma, Houston, Denver and many more places. We also played at The Winterland, San Francisco, where I had previously played with Tranquility. The hotel in Seattle called The Edgewater Inn where we stayed on 17th June was right on the sea front. We hired fishing rods from the hotel reception and fished out of the hotel windows. We mainly caught mud sharks which we held in the bath. Big Brian caught another type of fish which the hotel cooked for him.

The tour finished at the Sports Centre, San Diego, California on 22nd June. We had played 31 shows. By now the touring was starting to make me homesick. I loved the playing side but missed Goldie. I had smoked more weed than I should but it was to relax after shows; however I was concerned that it was too much and I am not even a smoker.

I was feeling tired and quite low at times. In the three years since we had been married I had been away in America for twelve months. The longest tour was with Tranquility for 12 weeks. That was a long tour. The travelling takes its toll more than the playing. It was not fair on Goldie either. I told her when we got married that my playing would always come first, and bless her she never moaned once. I hate it when musicians stop playing because their wives or girlfriends do not like it. You should never stop another person doing something they enjoy. This is only a disaster for a relationship.

Band members were moving on to other things and Maggie was keen to audition for replacements. I had no enthusiasm for it and told Maggie I was going to have a break for a while and from music altogether. And that is exactly what I did.

142

Chapter 9

'Time Out', Country Shack/ Gypsy/ Jackson Queen, Local Bands

At 5.30 p.m. on Sunday 3rd August 1975 I started a job on the night shift at Goldhanger Fruit Farms, a food canning factory. I also did day shifts of 6 am to 2 pm and 2 pm to 10 pm. I worked there for seven years. People working there would ask me what on earth was I doing working in place like that. During the busy summer season a lot of the workers were students.

Goldie and I had read a book by John Seymour about life in the country and being self-sufficient. We decided that we wanted to keep livestock and grow our own food. We started looking for a property with some land and eventually in the summer of 1976 found a fairly new end of terrace house with about an acre and a half at Tollesbury. Work mates at the factory thought we were mad having a mortgage as most of them lived in rented accommodation.

The day shifts at the factory gave me time at home while Goldie worked at City University in London as a secretary. When the peas were being canned everyone was walking around with green hands and spots of green on their faces from the ingredients being used. What was funny to me was labels would be changed for a different brand but it was all the same food, only Heinz had their own ingredients.

I eventually got one of the best jobs in the factory on the retorts which were giant pressure cookers that cooked hundreds of cans at once. Each cooker was about 8 foot deep. Baskets full of cans were winched into each cooker then the clamps would be turned and hit with 6 inch iron bars. We would wear ear defenders as it was very loud and hot with about 24 cookers on the go. There were two bays with cookers in each and four men would work in each area.

Having never really had a day job it was a bit of a novelty to me. I was made up to charge hand. I think they would have liked me to be a foreman but I enjoyed getting my hands dirty and working not walking around all day in a white coat. Bob Noble was one of the foremen. He was a small man who looked like Mr. Magoo with his white hard hat. He was a great laugh, a bit like Mr. Mackay from Porridge. He was always catching people smoking in the toilets. They would spend as much time as they could in there. He would shout at them and they would come running out from all directions. It was hilarious to watch. It would amaze me how many people were so lazy.

To Goldie's dismay I sold my Ludwig kit to one of my students, Richard, but it was on the proviso that if he ever wanted to sell it I would have first refusal. Which is what happened some years later. I nearly sold the Trixon kit but Goldie said that was a step too far. It was hard not playing. Hearing the music on the juke box in the factory canteen always made me feel I wanted to play again. Richard who had bought my kit worked on the retorts with me so music was always being discussed.

Things were progressing at Tollesbury; we had cleared a lot of the field and installed a chicken run and bought 12 Rhode Island Red chickens. It was great to have our own eggs. We bought some old pig huts and used them to house Nicky the goat. Rob and Kathy, our neighbours across the road were great fun and Rob had helped me with the huts. We also bought a large wooden and corrugated iron barn. The only problem was we had to dismantle it from a site in Colchester. We enlisted the help of our friends Tim and Carol who had bought our house in Silver End to move it. I asked Rob if he would help me erect the barn. He thought it was a small shed so you can imagine his face when he saw the size of it. Roundabout that time there was a Monty Python sketch on TV about Arthur Two Sheds Jackson, I became known as Three Sheds Francis!

One of the chaps I worked with had a Jersey cow which he had bought from a local farm. They culled out the ones which were not producing enough milk or were barren and they usually went to market for the slaughter trade. We went to see the farmer and he had one which kept getting mastitis in one of her udder quarters because she had a wonky teat which was difficult to milk . We bought her and called her Lillian, or Fag Ash Lil.

Lil was a lovely animal, very friendly with big brown eyes, teddy bear ears and a raspy tongue like sandpaper. She produced about 3 gallons of milk a day in two milkings. The milk was cooled and placed in a large bowl in the fridge and left to settle for 12 hours, then we could skim off the cream. It was like the skin in paint pots, really thick and we would get a couple of pints of it a day. We used the cream to make butter which was a bright yellow in the summer months.

We used to barter the milk with friends and neighbours as we were not allowed to sell it. One lady would do a couple of hours cleaning and ironing a week in return for milk and eggs. We put the goat's milk into cartons and froze it. We would sell some of it to a hospital for patients who were intolerant to cow's milk.

One day I had a call from Pete Brown who co-wrote hits with Jack Bruce for Cream. He had heard a recording I had made and wanted me to join his band, but I declined. He did phone a second time but I was adamant I needed a break.

After a break from playing of about a year I was approached by some musicians in the village to have a play with them. It felt good to be doing music again. I know my dad was upset when I stopped. The band went out as Rita and The Relatives (as most of them were). A good fun name. We played the odd gig in local pubs and village halls; no mammoth tours.

Whilst working with The Relatives Paul Argent put me in touch with a band called T-Bone. Paul worked in quality control at the canning factory. He used to play drums for them but had given up due to lack of time as he was also keeping pigs. I joined them and we played a lot of Status Quo material which went down well. They also had more work but it was still low key mainly village halls and parties. They were based in Burnham-on-Crouch which was about a forty minute drive from ours. We did one recording under the name of Citizens Arrest. I did not like the name T-Bone. The recording was never released.

I also did a session for Dave Brown as a special favour using my Trixon kit.

In October 1979 I received a call with information about a country band in need of a drummer. The band was called Country Shack and they had built up a good reputation for themselves on the country circuit. I went along for an audition. This was a different style of music for me but I enjoyed it. We had supported The New Riders of the Purple Sage, a country band, on one of the American tours and I liked their act.

The line up was Dick Gowers on bass, Terry Worlledge who ran the band and played guitar, Jenny Speller on vocals and Dave Hartley on pedal steel. They had a fan club which was run by Jan Woodhouse. This was a much more professional unit although everyone still had jobs and there was a lot of work around the country clubs. They all got along well. I joined and cut my hours down at the factory to four hours a day. This gave me time to concentrate on the music. I really had nothing in common with most of the work force there so it came at a good time for me to start pulling out.

The band did a lot of travelling up and down the country and had a group van and a roadie, Derek Guppy. Derek was not on the payroll but did the job because he really liked the band. Country Shack were voted the Most Promising Act in the Country 1980 and the most Popular Band to appear on Radio 2's Country Club. In 1980 we did an 8 day tour of the West Country and 10 days in Scotland.

Jenny left at the beginning of 1981 and Irene Lesley joined on lead vocals. In March Country Shack were booked to tour the UK supporting an American country star called Moe Bandy. Also on the tour were Dottsy and Roy Drusky. We backed Roy during the tour which was for 16 dates around the U.K. including the Wembley Festival.

Radio 2 favourite Shack brings an international air

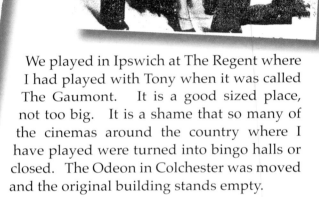

A BAND with an international following comes to Sittingbourne Town Hall for the first time next Wednesday as guest of the Jubilee Trail Country Music Club.

Country Shack, a five-piece band enhanced its international reputation recently by being voted most popular band to appear on B.B.C. Radio 2's "Country Club."

It can often be heard on the Thursday night programme and features three of its most requested tracks on an album released by the radio station.

Shack has earned its reputation as one of Britain's top country bands, travelling widely throughout the U.K. and on the continent and backing up live shows with appearances on both major television channels.

Lead guitarist Terry Worlledge is the longest serving member, now in his ninth year. Two recent changes to the line-up have revitalized the sound and instilled new enthusiasm.

Drummer Paul Francis has travelled the world with top international artists like Rolf Harris, Gilbert O'Sullivan and Maggie Bell (of Stone the Crows).

Another new face is steel guitarist, David Hartley.

Lead vocalist Jenny Speller was recently voted "top British female country singer" in a poll by Radio Oxford listeners.

Highlights of the act are Jenny's duets with Terry. He also does solo vocal spots and plays the harmonica.

Bassist Dick Gowers is the one to watch for snappy punch lines and, apparently, the best bass picking in the country.

Shack has two albums on the Sweet and Country label — "Portrait" and "Which Way Is Gone".

Supporting act to Shack is well-known and popular Medway group The J. C. Country Band.

We played in Ipswich at The Regent where I had played with Tony when it was called The Gaumont. It is a good sized place, not too big. It is a shame that so many of the cinemas around the country where I have played were turned into bingo halls or closed. The Odeon in Colchester was moved and the original building stands empty.

The tour with Moe went down well. On the last night in Yarmouth Dick our bass player walked on stage during Moe's act wearing a baby grow and sweeping the stage with a broom. It took Moe a little while to get used to the British sense of humour, but once he did he loved it.

He had a good tight band with him called The Rodeo Clowns. The guitarist had a party piece trick. We were all having a drink at the hotel one night after the show. In the centre of the table where we were sitting was an ashtray full of cigarette butts and ash. He asked how much we would give him to eat the lot. We told him not to be

Shack's star tour

ESSEX group Country Shack have begun a major nationwide tour as support to American country star Moe Bandy.

Led by lead guitarist and founder member Terry Worlledge of Oak Walk, Sible Hedingham, near Halstead, the band's tour coincides with their tenth anniversary.

During that decade, the group have achieved success few bands could hope to equal, including working for both TV networks, national and international radio, making records and a radio commercial, and winning many major awards.

Recently the group were voted the British Country Music Association's most promising act of 1980, and they are still the most popular band ever to appear on BBC Radio 2's Country Club programme.

Venues for the British tour this month, which also stars American artistes Dottsy and Roy Drusky, include the Ipswich Gaumont tomorrow, and an appearance at the Wembley Conference Centre on Sunday, March 22.

Some of the performances, including one at Peterborough, will be recorded for local radio.

Other members of the band include bassist Dick Gowers from Avon Way, Greenstead Estate, Colchester, and drummer Paul Francis from Tollesbury.

Country Shack also feature one of the finest young steel guitarists in the business, David Hartley from Thetford, and their newest member, lead vocalist Irene Lesley from Takeley.

• Country Shack line-up, left to right, back Paul Francis, Irene Lesley, Dick Gowers, front Terry Worlledge and David Hartley.

silly and he replied that he was serious. The rest of his band just smiled, they had obviously heard this all before. One of our band said a fiver but he said no it had to be worthwhile. Someone said that we should each put in a fiver. Once agreed he tipped some beer into the ashtray and downed the lot, chewing on the cigarette butts. It really turned your stomach to watch. I would not do that for £30, but he had no problem and it paid for his beer so he was happy.

The tour was over quickly compared to the marathons I had been used to in America. It was back to playing the country clubs. Mildenhall air base was always a good gig as they played the latest tracks from America including country rock which I liked. I never did go much on the slow Home on the Range material. The audiences always enjoyed themselves and that was good for us but I could never take seriously the guy in the audience dressed as an Indian complete with headdress, or dressed as an American soldier with his blanket strapped to his back and a toy rifle! But hey! They enjoyed themselves, so good luck to them.

We would get requested to play the American Trilogy with Elvis singing. We always said sorry we did not do that. It was at the end of the evening and as we made our way to the dressing room we could hear the rifles going off and we would fall about laughing. Not at the song, just the way the people would react.

In 1982 after six years in Tollesbury we decided that we would like to have a property with more land and somewhere where we would be settled for a long time. I phoned round the estate agents to see if there was anything we could afford and basically they said no. Then one phoned back to say a property with about 5 acres in Great Horkesley near Colchester had just come on the market. There were no printed details but we could view it.

It was a two bedroom bungalow which had been used as a smallholding. However it was quite run down and the greenhouses and polytunnels were in a sad state. The main field was overgrown with weeds nearly waist high and the owner was using it to race old bangers. But we both knew it would be ideal with a bit of TLC. We made an offer which was accepted.

Moving was quite a feat with all the animals. I went over just before the completion date and converted an old outbuilding into a stable for the cow and goat. Because there was no grass we grazed the cow on the back lawn until we got the main field ploughed and seeded and fenced.

Once again people at the factory thought I was mad taking on a large mortgage but we knew that houses with land were getting rarer to find. In August 1982 a couple of months after moving I was at work when I was asked to sweep an area. It was first thing in the morning and people were doing odd jobs until the production line started. The foreman who gave me the job enquired if I had done it and I said that I had. This was a foreman who hated getting his hands dirty and had no respect from the work force. He then told me to do it again.

Well, the one thing Geoff and I have in common is a quick temper. Something dad had if someone or some thing upset him. I think my grandfather was the same. I told this chap he could stick his broom up his arse and the job as well and walked out with everyone cheering. He actually did me a favour because I now had time to concentrate on my music. I had plenty of gigs and was teaching again in the spare bedroom.

We also had good outbuildings and a huge blue tractor. I had never seen such huge tyres. It was great driving it but it had a vicious clutch and I nearly went through the shed wall once. It also needed quite a lot of work and then water was getting into the oil, so we sold it.

We grew vegetables on about half an acre and sold them to a wholesaler. There was a small plantation of Christmas trees which was a good cash crop every year and we always replanted.

My dad loved it and was always pottering about. He set up a shop in one of the small sheds, selling fruit and veg and one week took about £90. We had many fruit trees, plum, greengage, eating and cooking apples, soft fruit and lots of different veg. Runner beans were always popular as were the Victoria Plums. We put a sign at the top of the road and people soon got to know us.

I remember when I was with Tony Jackson being interviewed and asked what was my ambition. I said apart from doing well in music I also wanted to own a house in the country with some land. So it had all happened. We were really chuffed to be living in such a lovely spot, rural yet close enough to the town and railway station. Goldie was still working in London.

Everything was going well until my whole world fell apart on 14th May 1984. In the early hours of the morning my brother Geoff telephoned to tell dad had died. He had had a heart attack. Goldie answered the phone and I could tell by her voice that something was wrong. I nearly fell over when she passed me the phone and Geoff told me. I had to sit down and pass the phone back to Goldie. Then I asked what had happended.

Mum and dad were at the chalet in Swalecliffe. Dad woke up about 1.30 a.m and said it was very hot. Mum got out of bed to either open a window or get some water when she heard dad sigh and that was it. Poor mum had to run down the lane to the house where the site manager and his wife lived. They called an ambulance but there was nothing they could do. Dad always looked so well. When people were told they could not believe it.

Dad was a fantastic father to Geoff and me and a good husband to mum. I could not take it in that he was no longer with us. It was very upsetting for the whole family. Goldie and I drove down to Geoff's. He had collected mum and brought her to his house in Rainham, Kent. Dad was taken to a hospital morgue. Poor mum looked so lost, it was terrible. We sat around waiting until morning then Geoff and I went to the hospital to identify dad. A policeman took us to the small hospital chapel. Dad just looked as though he was asleep. The officer was very kind. Poor Geoff signed the papers; his hand was shaking as he signed the death certificate.

We also went to the chalet and sorted out dad's clothes and belongings into a bag. It felt so bad seeing the clothes dad had worn that day.   Eventually the funeral was arranged and dad was buried in a small churchyard near Geoff in Kent. It was a lovely service and we went back to Geoff's. About an hour later I returned to the churchyard with my nephew Paul to read the messages and look at the lovely flowers.

Memories came flooding back. Dad had always been there for us. One Christmas mum sent dad and me out to buy the turkey.   As we walked past a music shop I pointed to a cymbal telling dad that was just what I needed. Bless him, he went in and bought it and we took home a chicken much to mum's disgust!

Back in Colchester I found it very hard to carry on with things. The veg garden became a chore and we were not making any money from keeping the various livestock, so we decided that it was time to quit the Good Life and just enjoy what we had.   Lessons were building up and we converted one of the outbuildings into a studio.   A couple of years later we converted another building into a rehearsal studio.

In 1985 Country Shack eventually regrouped and a new band called Gypsy was formed. We had Terry, me plus Taffy on bass, Janet Stevens vocals and Jan Woodhouse on keyboards. Having the two girls in the band worked well.   They sang well and were visually good for the band.

Taffy and Janet had worked together and when we auditioned Taffy for the bass player Janet came along just to watch.   It came out that she sang and when we heard her we could not believe our luck finding them both in one audition.

The material was a lot more upbeat and the vocals sounded really good. Another thing that we hated was certain clubs wanting to hear the same songs every gig. They would hand you a list of the numbers they wanted played. No way. We never went down that road and we did get negative comments from those places. The more forward clubs loved the band and they far outweighed the negative ones.

We were also asked to back well-known American artists at Wembley Arena. The shows were televised and went out on BBC 2 and radio to over 35 countries. We did several appearances at the Silk Cut Country Festival at Wembley in 1985 and 1986 backing Rex Allen Jnr and Roy Drusky plus spots on our own.

I enjoyed working with Jan and Taffy. When it came to loading up the van after a gig Jan would get stuck in helping carry the equipment. We laughed once to see Taffy under an umbrella sheltering from the rain and Jan carrying all the amps getting soaked.

Wembley date this Easter for Gypsy

Gypsy to play with the superstars.

TOP Essex group Gypsy will be making no less than three appearances at the Easter Silk Cut country music festival at Wembley which is now one of the biggest and most prestigius music events in the world.

Among the superstars featured on this year's show are Johny Cash, George Jones, Marie Osmond and a host of top international and American artists including Rex Allen Jnr with whom Gypsy take the main stage on Sunday night.

That performance will later be seen by millions of viewers when television recordings are screened in 35 countries worldwide.

Gypsy have also been selected to perform at the Best of British country music shows on Saturday and Monday. These shows represent the very best that Britain has to offer the world of country music and features acts from all over Britain, Ireland and the Channel Islands.

Gypsy — comprising of lead vocalist Janet Stephens and bassist Taffy Edwards, from Loughton, Jan Wood-house from Great Dunmow on keyboards, Terry Worledge, from Sible Hedingham on guitar and drummer Paul Francis from Great Horkesley — have a "soft spot" for Wembley. It was there that they made their first appearance together a year ago.

TRACK RECORD

The five-piece outfit was formed to provide backing for some of the stars at last year's festival but the band worked so well they have been together ever since.

Terry and Jan were formely part of Country Shack and are well known to country music fans. Janet and Taffy had a long stint with a band called Flair, winner's of TV's New Faces, and worked continually in Europe, Scandinavia and America, the home of the country music scene.

Paul also has a good track record, drumming his way round the world, performing and recording with many stars, including Bill Wyman, of the Rolling Stones, Rolf Harris, Gilbert O'Sullivan, Maggie Bell and Marion Montgomery.

After a good run with that line up, Jan and Taffy left in the summer of 1986. Roy Emney joined us on bass and we teamed up with an Irish lady called Tina James at the end of 1986 and she was the lead singer for a year. In November 1987 Julie Hester took over on vocals and we decided to change the name to Jackson Queen. Roy left and was replaced with Ken Elson. We played in The Best of British at Wembley at Easter 1988. Ken left the band and was replaced by Rob Stacey on bass. The band carried on for about a year until various members including myself decided to leave. My last gig with them was on 17th June 1990. Terry and Jan continued working as Jackson Queen.

Sadly Ken died several years later. Ken used to play in a band called Fusion with Nik Kershaw. Nik turned up for the funeral which was nice. Ken was such an intelligent person but always lived on the edge and was involved with drugs for a while. It was such a shame as he was a great bass player and far too young to die. When his coffin was carried into the church I felt so sad. There is always a strong bond between the bass player and drummer. After the service on the way home Goldie and I bought a tree to plant in our garden in his memory. All the musicians miss him. Apart from his great playing he was such a nice man.

151

The drum school was building up well and in 1986 I wrote my first drum tuition book Rhythmical Exercises for the Kit Player.   In 1988 I brought out two drum tuition videos 'The Complete Beginner' and 'Rhythmical Update'.

During the years 1982 to 1990 I played with many different local musicians in a variety of line ups.   Including the country gigs I was often out gigging 3 to 4 nights a week.   There were duos, trios, bands of various sizes including Contraband, Two's Company, The Diggeroos, Final Demand, Two Can, Flashback, Robbie Gladwell Band, Airey's Allstars, Harlequin, Steve Linton Band plus a Trad Jazz Band.

Working with a Trad Jazz Band was great fun and we played a regular gig at The Chequers pub at Goldhanger near Maldon.   I think it cost me more in petrol and a drink than I was paid but it was not about the money.   The other players were all good musicians and it was a fun gig to do.   The female vocalist had an excellent voice, and the sound of the trombone was great.

On 15th February 1987 Final Demand supported the Steve Marriott Band at The Works in Colchester and again on 16th June 1988 I played in the Robbie Gladwell Band at the Oliver Twist supporting Steve.

I also did a gig in September 1988 for Tim Mann in Norwich backing Craig Douglas who had a big hit with 'Only Sixteen' in 1959 and 'When My Little Girl is Smiling' in 1962.

On 24th April 1990 I did my first drum clinic with Terry Chimes (ex Clash) at the Colchester Arts Centre.

Chapter 10

1990-1996 Steve Harley & Cockney Rebel

In May 1990 I received a call from Robbie Gladwell saying he was going to start work with Steve Harley and be part of his band. Steve had hits in the 70's as Steve Harley and Cockney Rebel. He needed a drummer and Robbie asked if I was interested. I mean, is the Pope a Catholic? A definite Yes was the reply.

Steve and I arranged to meet on 15th May in a pub in Suffolk near where he lived. We had a good chat about my career and what he wanted from me. Steve came over to the studio one day with a guitar and we played over some of his songs. He gave me copies of his material to learn. The only problem was time as Goldie and I were off on holiday to Scotland for five days to visit our friends Tony and Joyce in Thurso. I spent the journeys and any spare time listening to the tracks as time was of the essence.

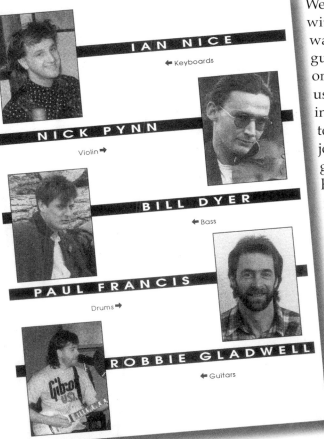

IAN NICE
← Keyboards

NICK PYNN
Violin →

BILL DYER
← Bass

PAUL FRANCIS
Drums →

ROBBIE GLADWELL
← Guitars

We had about four rehearsals in my studio with the full band. Steve's brother Ian was on keyboards and Nick Pynn on guitar and violin. Robbie Gladwell was on guitar and Rob Stacy did rehearse with us but again because of his job which was in his father's printing firm decided not to go into music full-time. Billy Dyer joined the band on bass. Billy had a great feel and the band all got on well. I had heard Steve's hits but not the album material. We played it as close to the record as we could but as time went on Steve encouraged everyone to be themselves.

The first gig on 3rd June was in Nurenburg, Germany, to eleven thousand people. As well as the band Steve employed eight crew members. There was Roy Wood the sound engineer and Dave Thomas as back line technician. This meant that I had my drums set up for me which was fantastic. It was a real treat to play a gig and come off and not have to go back and pack away the kit. Dave was never far away and if I needed anything it was there. A snare head went one night and Dave came on with a spare drum and changed them over. Steve never knew until after the show as Dave had changed it so quickly. He was a really good drum tech.

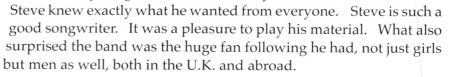

We had 19 U.K. dates from 5th June until 11th July and 27 dates on the European tour from 14th October until 19th November. We all travelled in a coach. John Magna was the tour manager. There was a stage monitor engineer so the sound the band had in the monitors was different to front house. We also had a lighting engineer.

The drums were set up on a big riser stage right and the keyboards were on a riser stage left. Ian and I would look over and watch Steve for any cues to stop a number or punctuate a section with bass drum or keyboard. Steve could stop at any point so you had to be ready. Each gig was different. The job with Steve was a big step up for me career-wise. Everything had to run smoothly as Steve knew exactly what he wanted from everyone. Steve is such a good songwriter. It was a pleasure to play his material. What also surprised the band was the huge fan following he had, not just girls but men as well, both in the U.K. and abroad.

In 1991 we played 16 dates in the U.K. and Europe. Steve had tracks already in the can for a new CD but needed a few more to finish it off. Simon Phillips, the drummer, had a studio at his house, The White House in Bures, Suffolk. Steve booked this for recording in November 1991. This was great for me as it was only a few miles away.

Simon is a great player with excellent studio knowledge. It was good talking about our collections of snare drums and what sounded best. My Sonorlite kit always sounded good live or in the studio. I got that kit about the same time I started my endorsement with Zildjian cymbals. For the touring I had to invest in some seriously heavy duty cases to protect the kit and cymbals.

I played on 3 tracks on the Yes You Can CD: 'Star for a Week ('dino')', 'The Alibi', and 'New-Fashioned Way'. Alan Darby played guitar on some tracks and was to do some dates with us then Milton McDonald took over from him.

On 3rd February 1992 we did a live TV show in Frankfurt Music Hall. The CD was released in 1992 and the Yes You Can European 13 date tour started in Hanover on 7th March and ended on 22nd in Berlin plus one gig on 19th April at the Windo Rock Festival in Belgium. We visited Switzerland, Holland, Vienna, Belgium and good old Hamburg where just about anything goes on. The band went to a sex show out of boredom and nearly got thrown out for heckling. It was funny.

The German coach was amazing. It had beds, a small kitchen and a loo. The back half was fitted out like a big lounge with a TV. On the British leg of the tour there were even small practice amps on board. We only slept on the coach once which was when we travelled to Vienna

WINDO-ROCK, BELGIUM   19 APRIL 1992

overnight so that we would have a day off there. The first time we played there we arrived, set up, did the show then left early the next day, so it was good to have a bit of time there.

In Germany one night after a show we were eating out in a restaurant when a diner recognised Steve. He was a big fan and asked if he could buy Steve a drink. Steve said that red wine would be nice. He bought Steve a bottle of red wine costing about £300 and the fan only drank beer!

The one thing Steve has is high standards. At one gig in Germany we needed to take a leak. There were no toilets or facilities to wash available in the dressing room. The promoter told Steve the toilets were next door. Steve replied that these were public toilets. He told the promoter that he would not use these as people had paid to come and see him perform not find him in the toilet standing next to them.

The promoter was asked to fetch a dustbin and bin liners, hot water, soap and towels. We put the bin liners in the dustbin and peed in that. How some of these so called promoters treat artists is amazing. If I went to see The Shadows I would never expect to find Hank Marvin in a public loo. Some people really don't have a clue. The same applies to artists as well. I think they should make an effort to look smart and tidy not go on stage in jeans that look like they have been slept in.

I enjoyed the enthusiasm of the crowds in Europe. At one show the lorry carrying the equipment had a problem which made it very late arriving at the gig. We were already there in the dressing room. The audience were let in and came running down to the front of the stage. It was great to see their reaction as there was no equipment set up on stage; it was empty. It finally arrived about half an hour from show time. All the band helped get it in and set up. The show turned out to be really good.

The 21 date U.K. Yes You Can Tour started on 1st May in Bradford and ended in Newcastle on 28th May.

As with any act certain countries or areas are particularly good. Manchester, London and Leeds were great for Steve in the U.K. When we did get to play Manchester Steve warned us that the audience would be enthusiastic. The building was packed solid and there was no way we could walk through the crowd so we had to leave the building and walk round to an exit door to get on stage. Once that door opened the crowd all cheered.

Usually to open the show we had the lights down and a segment of music from The Mission playing. I loved walking on stage to that music. Once everyone was in place the lights would go up and we were straight into the first number. The show went really well and they were a great audience. Leaving the building after the show we made a dash back to the dressing room at the rear of the hall.

On the Yes You Can tours we had a German band supporting us called Fury and The Slaughterhouse. At the Manchester venue when the equipment was being broken down and loaded into vehicles their huge mixing desk worth thousands of pounds was stolen. We are talking about a big piece of equipment and it would take two people or more to carry it. We were amazed that they had the nerve to do it under everybody's noses.

I loved playing the theatres. As I stood in the wings and looked at my kit with the stage lights on it the buzz was amazing. It looked so good and I could not wait to sit behind it and play. When you have good stage lighting it makes such a difference to a show.

On one occasion when we had finished playing we had to get out of the hall through the kitchen so that Steve would not get set upon by his fans. Once out in the street we hailed two cabs to take us to the hotel. The fans were running down the road after the cabs. Steve has very loyal fans.

This came in handy for me when I had to renew my passport. I went to the passport office in Peterborough. At this time I still had the original black British passport and I wanted another one the same. I did not like the idea of having a red European one. I asked the man at the desk if it would be possible to have the black one and he told me that they were being phased out and all the new ones were the red European passports.

He looked at the old passport and the forms and noticed that I was a musician. He asked if I worked for anyone well known. I told him I was working with Steve Harley and Cockney Rebel. Well, the guy nearly fell off his chair. It turned out that he was a huge fan of Steve and with that he said he thought he would be able to find an old style passport for me! True to his word he did and I was well chuffed to get a black British passport. It had made his day to meet me and he had a huge grin across his face as I left.

We played various other dates in 1992 and 1993 including a 10 date U.K. tour. There were a few gigs in 1994 and 1995 including a TV show in Antwerp. During the time I was with Steve each tour was well planned whether it was in the U.K. or Europe. We played at large festivals with other acts with crowds of 20,000 people. They were good fun. On 4th June 1994 we played at the Glamrock Festival in Esbjerg, Denmark. Headlining were

Deep Purple with Joe Satriani on guitar. Also on the bill were ELO, Status Quo, Smokie, Suzi Quatro and Bonnie Tyler. It was quite a line up. At another festival we had Gary Moore and Joan Jett and the Blackhearts. Once we filmed an hour long show in a huge tent for German TV. It looked like the circus had come to town.

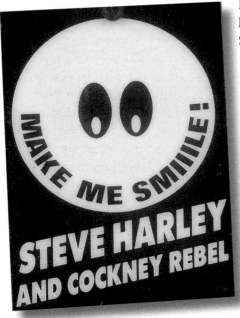

In May 1996 I recorded 9 tracks on Steve's CD called Poetic Justice. This was recorded in a great studio in Sussex. Berry House Studio had accommodation and food and we set up in the lounge. The sound was great. Andy Brown was on bass and we also worked with Phil Beer on guitar.

After a lot of consideration I decided to concentrate on the drum school and regrettably handed in my notice with Steve. I found him a replacement so at least that saved all the audition process for him. I was sorry to leave but it was hard juggling things about. I had learnt a lot whilst working with Steve, particularly communicating with the audience. I remember one festival abroad with many well-known artists. One in particular was on just before us. He had a great voice but no stage presence or connection with the audience. As soon as we came on Steve had them all on his side. These would be the things I would miss.

Chapter 11

1990-1996 Tony Jackson & The Vibrations, The Soul Detectives

In 1990 I came across a compilation album of various tracks and one was Tony Jackson and The Vibrations. On the sleeve notes it said that Tony was now managing a golf club in Nuneaton. This was a great opportunity to get in touch again. After contacting a few golf clubs I managed to get the right number. It was fantastic to talk again after over twenty years.

We arranged to meet up in London in a few weeks' time. At 11 a.m. on Thursday 10th May 1990 I met Tony outside the Tottenham pub in Oxford Street. I took a camera with me and got a passer-by to take a photo of us. We chatted for a couple of hours and said how good it would be to do some gigs.

Unfortunately Ian had died in 1987 of a brain haemorrhage. Tony was not aware of this and was very saddened by the news. I said I could put a band together and Tony said let's give it a go.

Above:
Tony and Paul meet after over 20 years. Thursday 10th May 1990, London

Right:
Chris, Paul, Tony, Fred, Rob

Far Right:
Steve, Tony, Fred, Paul, Chris

I enlisted Colin Free, or Fred as he is known, on guitar and Rob Stacy on bass and I found a keyboard player called Chris Teeder. Rob was tied up with his job so after a few months Steve English joined us on bass. We started rehearsing in my studio at Great Horkesley. It felt great playing the old numbers again, plus the big hits of The Searchers that Tony sang on.

We kept the same name of Tony Jackson and The Vibrations. At one point the name Tony Jackson's Researchers was mentioned but that went down like a pork chop in a synagogue. In the Searchers camp Mike Pender was already out on the road with his band called Mike Pender's Searchers.

Fred and I also did some gigs together and some recording for Janet Stevens, but it was the mark two version of Tony Jackson and The Vibrations that I really wanted to get off the ground. However, over the next couple of years this did not prove to be easy as I was very busy with Steve Harley and Cockney Rebel.

TONY JACKSON & THE VIBRATIONS

Well and truly BACK on the 60's scene, from the original line-up of legendary Liverpool group, THE SEARCHERS, we present TONY JACKSON - vocalist on such classic hits as "SWEETS FOR MY SWEET" "SUGAR AND SPICE"

During 1992 Tony appeared on shows with, among others, The Tremeloes, The Fortunes, The Merseybeats, The Swinging Blue Jeans and Mike McCartney, not to mention a long-awaited reunion concert with another original Searcher - Mike Pender, an event which Radio 2's Brian Matthew described as "UNMISSABLE" and which The Beat Goes On magazine called "THE BEST SHOW OF THE YEAR"

****

Tony Jackson together with his current band "The Vibrations" who comprise former members of Steve Harley's "Cockney Rebel" and Marty Wilde's "Wildcats" are available for one-nighters, tours and summer seasons during 1993

****

I also did a few gigs with Robbie Gladwell. Suzie Quatro, who lived locally, got up and did a few numbers at one which went really well and I enjoyed playing for her.

Our first gig with Tony was on 8th December 1990 in Enfield. The band was sounding good but we needed more work. The second gig was on 14th December in Camberley.

We only had a couple of gigs in 1991. The main one being a charity gig at The Embassy Suite, Colchester on 25th June. This was run by The Beat Goes On magazine for St. Helena's Hospice. The other gig was on 14th December at The Royal Chase Hotel, Enfield. The next gig was on 15th January 1992 at the Town Hall, Hammersmith.

Steve English left the band and was replaced by Billy Dyer who was also still working with Steve Harley.

Things picked up in the summer with Heywood Civic Hall, Manchester on 27th June, with The Swinging Blue Jeans.   There were six more gigs that year:

3rd October - The Beat Goes On Convention at the Stanley Halls, London.

23rd October - Sounds of the 60's with The Tremeloes and The Fortunes at the Concert Hall, Fairfield Halls, Croydon.

1st November - The Mersey Reunion with Mike Pender's Searchers and The Merseybeats at the Civic Hall, Guildford

22nd November - Parr Hall, Warrington with Mike Pender's Searchers

5th December - a private function at The Embassy Suite, Colchester

31st December - Heywood Civic Hall, Manchester

Supported by compatriots from the '60's "Cupid's Inspiration", Tony Jackson and The Vibrations topped the bill on New Year's Eve at the Heywood Civic Hall, near Manchester.

This large venue, a favourite haunt for many Sixties groups and fans alike, was soon rocking to the sounds of "Farmer John", "Love Potion No. 9" and "Watch Your Step".   When Tony decided to slow the pace down with a wistful "What Have They Done To The Rain" the audience complimented the occasion by listening intently, though Colin Free's "Get Back" and "Rise and Fall of Flingel Bunt" soon had them clapping hands and stomping feet in true New Year's Eve party tradition.   No, it wasn't "Auld Lang Syne" time yet if Tony had anything to do with it!

With a fine rendition of his first solo hit "Bye, Bye Baby" Tony again had them rocking in the aisles to Creedence Clearwaters' "Up Around The Bend" followed by his excellent soul versions of "All Right Now" and Sam and Dave's "Hold On I'm Comin'".

With the chimes of midnight upon us, Tony led "audience participation time" through that famous anthem "You'll Never Walk Alone" (eat your heart out, Gerry), a finale which eventually led to Tony being called back on stage three times, (it's okay, here's a song we prepared earlier!!!!).

It should be observed that The Vibrations are an extremely tight, talented band,   with bass player Billy Dyer enjoying himself immensely, and band comedian Colin "Fred" Free always ready with a one-liner.   Original "Vibe" Paul Francis is generally accepted to be arguably the best '60's percussionist around, and supple- ment all this with keyboard ace Chris Teeder - show me where you were on New Year's Eve!

I was quite surprised to see how many of the 60's bands still gigged.   Some artists have worn well while others you would have a job to know who they were.   Billie Davis got in touch and asked if we could back her on a show that Tony was doing.   She came down to my studio and we ran through some numbers but Tony was not keen on us backing another artist so we just did our show.

The show at the Civic Hall, Guildford, on 1st November 1992 had Mike Pender's Searchers, Tony Jackson and The Vibrations, the Mersey Beats with a reunion of Tony Crane and Billy Kinsley.   Mike McCartney from Scaffold was also on the bill.   Tony also sang a couple of numbers with Mike Pender which was the first time in over twenty years since Tony had left the Searchers.   They had a great response and watching from the front it was evident what an integral part of the Searchers they were.

On one show a well known vocalist got stuck in a toilet cubicle with a lady and was calling for help for someone to open the door. You had to laugh. If it had happened in the 60's he would have jumped over the door.

In 1993 Fred and I decided to run two versions of the band; one doing the 60's and the other playing a variety of material. Graham Neville, or Grip as he is known, joined us on vocals. We decided to concentrate on Soul and Latin numbers. Chris came up with the name The Soul Detectives. It felt good playing more varied material.

The one and only gig in 1993 was on 22nd August when Tony Jackson and the Vibrations and The Soul Detectives had a gig at The Victory pub in West Mersea, Colchester. It had a big marquee attached to the pub. Tony turned up early in the day and was staying at the pub. Unfortunately fans started buying him drinks during the day. We had an audience of about 400 people but by the time Tony was due to go on he was the worse for wear due to the drink.

The Soul Detectives played a good set. Grip had a great soulful voice. After the interval we got ready to introduce Tony. The stage was only about a foot high. Tony put one foot on then fell backwards onto the floor. His head only missed the PA speaker by inches. He got up and this time made it onto the stage. The only trouble was he could not stand still and he came backwards towards the drum kit. I stopped playing and pushed him forwards and he grabbed hold of an iron bar which was part of the marquee frame and hung there. There was no way he could sing.

Grip had fled to the loo and stayed in there. Goldie called him and said the band would have to finish without Tony. I got off the kit and asked Billy to help me take the mic from Tony. I don't know what the audience were thinking. We finished the show and when I was paid I gave Tony his share even though he had not sung. I told him I could not work with him anymore until he sorted himself out. We had only done about 13 gigs. From that day on the band just worked as The Soul Detectives. I kept in touch with Tony; we often spoke on the phone. Over the next few years he did the odd guest appearance with the Rapiers. It broke my heart to see him in such a bad way.

In 1993 I received a call one day from Suzi Quatro while she was in Germany asking if I was interested in a job with her as her drummer was leaving. I was in the middle of teaching when she rang so she said she would call the following day when she was back in the UK. To work with Suzi would mean that I would have to stop doing gigs with Tony and Steve plus my teaching would be affected so I declined the offer. I suggested she should try Andrew Dowding who was also teaching at Orchard Percussion. I also suggested Jim Ledbetter, a friend and former student whose father John also played drums. Jim was only 20 but was a very good drummer.

I asked Suzi to let me know how they both did so she called and said she had chosen Andy. Like me Andy has asthma and she was a bit concerned about this but I assured her that he would be fine. She had enjoyed Jim's playing but unfortunately he had his head down all the time and she needed visual contact to end the song!

In late 1993 I started work on a new drum tutor book. By the time it was nearly finished I was approached by a publishing company interested in putting it out. I signed with them and in 1994 Concentrating on Co-ordination was published. The book included a CD. The book was advertised in the drum magazines with full page colour adverts. To promote the book I did a string of drum clinics around Britain in association with Drummik (I endorsed their drum microphones) and The Soul Detectives also played at some of them.

It was at the Colchester clinic on 23rd June 1994 that I first met George Apoussidis who was the Sonor rep. George organised more clinics in Britain and Ireland. On the 7th February 1995 we did a clinic in Porthcawl, Wales, which had a really good turn out. We spent ages afterwards chatting and signing autographs. I had Chris Childs with me on bass. Chris had worked with Paul Young and Thunder.

On 30th April I returned to Porthcawl for another clinic accompanied by Lincoln Anderson on bass. From there we went to Ireland. Unfortunately the ferry crossing was really rough. I am not a particularly good sailor and felt ill for most of the crossing. To make matters worse once we had disembarked George drove very fast on the windy roads and that made me even sicker. The last thing I wanted to do was a drum clinic, but I soon recovered.

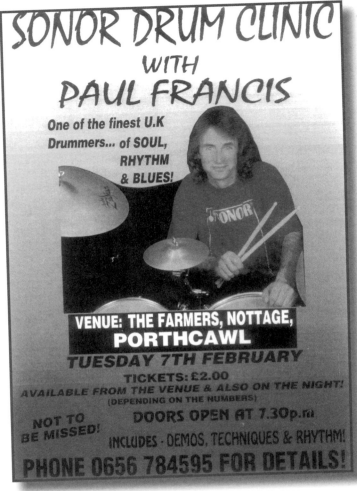

SONOR DRUM CLINIC
WITH
PAUL FRANCIS

One of the finest U.K
Drummers... of SOUL,
RHYTHM
& BLUES!

VENUE: THE FARMERS, NOTTAGE,
PORTHCAWL

TUESDAY 7TH FEBRUARY

TICKETS: £2.00
AVAILABLE FROM THE VENUE & ALSO ON THE NIGHT!
(DEPENDING ON THE NUMBERS)

NOT TO
BE MISSED!

DOORS OPEN AT 7.30p.m

INCLUDES - DEMOS, TECHNIQUES & RHYTHM!

PHONE 0656 784595 FOR DETAILS!

The clinics in Ireland were also very well supported and 200 people attended the one in Cork. I really enjoyed the clinics in Ireland. At our last clinic the promoter who was the owner of the music shop asked if we could start earlier as a lot of the audience were drummers who had gigs to go to. This suited us fine as we had an early ferry to catch in the morning and we finished the clinic by nine o'clock.

The promoter asked us to go to an acoustic gig in a pub where he was playing. So we went along and had a great time but unfortunately it was very late before we got back to our B & B and we only had two hours before we had to leave. Fortunately we were all in one room with three single beds and somehow we managed to catch a little sleep before leaving on time. We had a very slow trip to the ferry feeling the worse for wear.

In February 1996 I did a series of eleven drum clinics in Ireland and England. This time I was accompanied by Andy Brown on bass who had also played with Steve Harley. At one clinic in Belfast we arrived thinking we had plenty of time, but there was already a large audience waiting. It was a bit awkward setting up with so many people in the shop. No one offered us a drink on arrival, so after a while I asked for one. I was given water in a cracked cup and that was it! However the clinic went really well. Most of the time we were very well looked after. I really enjoyed my Irish experience and the Irish people.

When people at the clinics asked me to sign a copy of my book it made me feel very proud and I know my dad would have loved it. The clinic at Colchester Art Centre was recorded and put out on video 'Live In Clinic'.

Chapter 12

The Soul Detectives, Tony Jackson, Jack Bruce, Jet Harris

In 1995 Grip and Billy decided to move on and were replaced with Darren Davis on vocals and Mick Nottage on bass. We managed to poach Darren away from another soul band that was not doing much work. Mick and Darren fitted in really well.

Darren had worked in holiday camps and was brilliant with talking to the audience. He also had a great voice so we were very lucky. Mick had a good feel and played some great slap bass Mark King style. So we were up and running again. We built up a strong following round the pubs. They would get packed solid and you could hardly move. We also did functions. Darren has a great sense of humour. He and I would spot someone in the audience who looked like a well-known person, or if somebody slipped or fell over due to drink, Darren would blow his whistle which would crack me up. We would both then be in fits of laughter. A cow bell was also used if someone played a wrong chord or messed something up; that got a lot of use! We laughed a lot when we saw the funny side of things, but we took the music seriously.

Darren had started in the music business as a drummer then switched to lead vocals. I thought it a good idea to give him some percussion bits to play out front. Darren's wife Debbie bought him some timbales and I found a splash cymbal and various bits and pieces plus a cow bell. Now we had two for when things went wrong! Darren was playing good parts and not just random bits and the percussion really added to the sound.

In November 1995 keyboard player Tim Mann put a band together to back artists at a cabaret club in Newmarket and I was asked to play. The first night we backed Wee Willy Harris who had been a regular on the old TV shows like 6.5 Special. Then we backed Jimmy Jones the comedian. The last two nights we backed a female vocalist then Joe Pasquale. He was a modern day Tommy Cooper. He was great fun to work with. Doing two nights with him was such a laugh. I have some wooden puppets and Joe asked me to bring one in. I put it on the drums and he used it in his act. What was nice about him was the fact that he was so down to earth. He made us cups of tea and was so chuffed to be invited to do The Royal Variety Performance for the second time. He deserved his success and yes, he does talk in a high voice and it is not put on.

In November 1996 Tim and I promoted a gig at Colchester Charter Hall. It was with Jimmy Jones, the comedian, supported by The Soul Detectives.

In 1996 Tony Jackson got into trouble. He carried an artificial gun as he felt vulnerable when he went out because somebody had had a go at him. He felt he was not strong enough to defend himself. He had split from his wife, Linda, and had moved to Nottingham where he had an on off relationship with a lady called Margaret. One day he was in a phone box making a call when a woman outside the box kept opening the door asking him how long was he going to be. There was a heated exchange of words and Tony waved the fake gun at her. A passerby knocked the gun out of his hand and the Police were called. Tony was arrested and cautioned.

Some time later he went to the same phone box. The same woman was in the phone box. She panicked and called the Police thinking that Tony was after her. They apprehended Tony and found a small knife on him which he was carrying for protection. Tony was given 18 months in jail. The Judge was set on making an example of him but he was a very frail man with all sorts of medical problems. Jail was the wrong place to send him with hardened criminals.

He appealed but it was turned down. He would have to serve at least a year. Poor Tony was put in a cell with some hardened criminals. In one letter he said one cell mate was a drug addict and tried to intimidate Tony. It must have been hell for him. It really knocked the stuffing out of him. He said it had aged him by twenty years.

We kept up the correspondence and I tried to keep up his morale saying we could do more gigs once he was out of jail. But even Tony realised his health was deteriorating. He was worried he would lose his Council flat because of the payments. It was a right mess. He should never have left Linda; she was a lovely person. Christmas was a hard time for him. But he still kept his sense of humour.

Margaret, his girlfriend, did visit a few times at the beginning. I wanted to visit but Tony said it was not worth coming all that way for such a short visit, plus Margaret might be there. He was always pleased to receive all the news and asked about the band in his letters.

Eventually it was time for his release. He had served roughly a year of an eighteen month sentence. He was so pleased to be out. It is even worse for someone who has had fame as inmates can be very cruel. But I know some of them were on his side and liked his music so he did have some support.

Once out Tony and I kept in regular contact by phone. He got himself a cat and rarely went out mainly due to his failing health. Tony was a very good artist and loved sketching and painting. I have a really nice painting which he did. Tony had owned a flat in Spain but sold it to pay all the bills while inside. The painting has a very Spanish feel to it.

The Soul Detectives recorded their first CD 'Tracked' in 1996 which we sold at gigs.

In November 1997 the band had the opportunity to go to Gabon in Central Africa close to the equator. Chris had a brother who worked for Shell Oil and every year they had a good party with entertainment for the workers and their families. This year the theme was 60's, so we all dressed the part. It was really a paid holiday for us but too good an opportunity to miss. Mr. Nutty a children's entertainer from Colchester was also booked.

We flew to Libreville, the capital, then a short inland flight on a small aircraft to Port Gentil and another one to our destination Gamba. It was great looking out; treetops everywhere for miles and miles. Not a house in sight. It was fantastic. The Shell complex where the families lived was in the middle of nowhere; a clearing in the jungle. We all stayed in one of the bungalows on the site. The site had all mod cons with a huge

club house where we had our meals and played billiards. There was also a large swimming pool. Drums and backline were supplied so we only had to take guitars and keyboard. We played a short set for the children's party and Mr. Nutty entertained them. Our 60's gig went really well. Everyone had gone to a lot of trouble with the 60's theme and it was very colourful and a success.

Above: Darren, Paul, Fred, Mick, Chris

During our week's stay we were driven by lorry into the jungle to do a show in a works canteen. Some of the equipment went by river on a raft. We stayed in Portacabins where the work force lived. The show was a great success but it was strange just having an audience of men and seeing them dancing together. It was great driving along the dirt road with dense rain forest to either side. The road was only wide enough for one vehicle so they were timed as to when they could travel either way.

Back at the complex we had some days off so someone was put in charge of us and they took us to play golf and go fishing. We saw hippos and elephants in the wild which was an amazing experience.

In 1998 the band had a few changes. Chris left and was replaced by Mitch. We decided to include a brass section for a fuller sound and Darren Parker joined on sax and Johnny Tait on trumpet. Johnny did not stay long as he went to play on the ships so Grant Jones took his place.

The great thing was we had the opportunity to visit Gabon a second time in November 1999. Although Chris was no longer with the band he was keen for us to go again. Unfortunately Shell would not pay for a seven piece band so we went as the original Soul Detectives with Chris. This time the theme was the 70's and we hired some clothes for that one. Chris had a beard at the time and after our first set he shaved it off just leaving a Hitler moustache, then we went on and played a Sparks number. It was brilliant to see the reaction and look of surprise on the audience's faces.

Again we stayed in a bungalow. There were coconut trees in the garden and the gardener would cut them open for us with a machete. This time we had Dave to show us around and a 4 x 4 to drive about in. One day we went out to eat in a nearby village. The buildings were just wooden huts on earth floors. Unfortunately I was very ill the next day. We were in the car when I felt ill. It came on so quickly. I got out of the car, fell over and was sick. I could not stand up for a few minutes. I thought "here we go again, food poisoning". Luckily it was not as bad as the time in New York. A doctor on the complex fixed me up with some tablets. Poor Mick cannot stomach melted cheese on food and he had a job to find any food that was not covered in it.

I would tell the others to keep their cameras with them in case we saw an elephant then blow me down the one day I forgot mine one appeared on the piece of cleared land used for the landing strip. I did however manage to get some good footage on the video on a different occasion. We were sound checking when this man came in and said there was an elephant and a calf near by. He took me in his jeep and it was so good to see them and several others. We also had another chance when a big bull elephant was on the edge of the site. We got very close to it as it was standing in a ditch eating bananas. They are such wonderful animals. How people can kill them for their tusks is beyond me.

We saw quite a few monkeys during our stay but they were high in the trees swinging about.   All the roads were dirt tracks and once Shell Oil pulled out it would all revert back to forest which is nice.   We were told the site would be handed over to the Gabon government towards the end when they would use it and then close it down once the oil became harder to obtain.   We were so lucky to have the opportunity to go there.   Needless to say we had a lot of laughs while we were there.

The first day in the jungle camp we were shown into a Portacabin office to get the information.   The site manager told us to help ourselves to tea.   Fred went to get a cup and his camera slid off his shoulder smashing into the cups.   With that the chap who had a strong Yorkshire accent said "Fucking hell, is he always like that?   I hope he's insured."   Darren and I just lost it.   For the whole stay we would mimic that sentence.

Once home we were kept busy gigging including one at a Devon village festival.   The band had now been extended to a nine piece with the addition of two girl singers for backing vocals and the odd lead vocal.   Over the years various brass players left and were replaced.   One member, Grant Jones was in the Blues and Royals and could be seen in Trooping the Colour and other military displays.   He even got a name check on the TV in 2010 as Field Officer.   His wife Maria was one of the backing singers.   Eventually we cut back to one girl along with Darren on vocals.

In Aid of
The Bridge Project

STEVE
HARLEY
AND
COCKNEY
REBEL

With Special Guest
JACK BRUCE
Quay Theatre 3/10/99

Steve Harley called and asked if I would do a charity show in Sudbury at The Quay Theatre on 3rd October 1999.   It was with Jack Bruce as the guest doing some Cream material.   Steve would use his band for the first set then other players would make up a band for Jack.   This would include myself, with Steve and Robbie on guitar and Jack on bass.   Jack is a fantastic musician and songwriter so I was only too pleased to be asked.   We had a rehearsal at my studio.   We had only just started when a TV crew arrived to film it for the local news.   They were asked to take a tea break while we went over the material then it was filmed.

It went really well and everyone had a good time.   Jack's numbers with Cream have become classics.   It was fun to play them and also be on stage with Steve again.

The Soul Detectives put on their own shows at the Quay Theatre, Sudbury on 3rd September 1999 and again on 2nd November 2001. We also had a gig at the Princes Theatre in Clacton on Friday 17th August 2001. On the last two occasions Darren and I had worked out a

Above:
On stage in Sudbury with Steve, Jack and Robbie

routine together involving drum sticks that glowed in the dark. It was different and very effective and went down really well.

The band recorded their second CD 'When You're Ready' in 2000 and also added various female backing vocals for a couple of years. Tina Stevens joined the band as lead and backing vocals alongside Darren. Glyn Sweeting played trumpet 2002 – 2003 and was replaced by Tony Hawkins. In 2003 the 'Carry On RIGArdless' CD was recorded live at the Riga Music Bar.

I have been fortunate to have played with many good bass players during my career including Alan Jones who later went on to work with The Shadows. One day I noticed that Jet Harris the original bass player from The Shadows was gigging again. I managed to get in touch and asked him if he would like our band to back him at a small theatre in Sudbury. He said he would and it was arranged that The Soul Detectives would play the first

Left:
Paul and Jet Harris

QUAY THEATRE, SUDBURY
SATURDAY, 19TH FEBRUARY, 2000

JET HARRIS ex SHADOWS

ORIGINAL BASS GUITARIST WITH **CLIFF RICHARD AND THE SHADOWS.** HITS INCLUDE WONDERFUL LAND, HIGH CLASS BABY, FBI, DIAMONDS, SCARLET O'HARA, APPLEJACK AND MANY MORE. APPEARING WITH

THE SOUL DETECTIVES

FOLLOWING THEIR SELL-OUT PERFORMANCE LAST SEPTEMBER, THE SOUL DETECTIVES ONCE MORE SET THE QUAY'S STAGE REVERBERATING TO THE SOUND OF SOUL, LATIN AMERICAN AND OTHER EXCITING STYLES.

set then Jet would do the last set. He sent us a video tape to give us an idea of the numbers he would be doing.

Jet would be using his own keyboard player, Cliff Halls, who had done a lot of work with The Shadows over the years. My friend Chris Halls ex Colchester band Harlequin would play rhythm guitar. I booked the Quay Theatre, Sudbury for the evening of Saturday, 19th February 2000.

Jet and Cliff arrived the day before the gig and we rehearsed in my studio. We had all worked through our parts to make sure it went OK. I enjoyed working out the Tony Meehan parts. The rehearsal went well and Jet was pleased. He said it felt like playing with Tony Meehan again so I was well chuffed. We all went for a drink at the local pub and although Jet did not drink alcohol he enjoyed the pub and the conversation.

Our show the next evening went very well. Chris and I were big Shadows fans so it was great playing their material. I started out playing along to The Shadows in my brother's bedroom, now here we were backing Jet. It was a great experience. In fact it was as if I had gone full circle. Jet was really nice and that made it all the more special. Jet continued working until he died of throat cancer in March 2011, aged 71.

I had the pleasure of meeting The Shadows when Clem Cattini was on the same show with them at Caesars Palace, Luton. We chatted for about an hour after their show. It was nice to meet them. I have always enjoyed their music. Later on I went to Brian Bennett's house as he had various drum parts that he needed to get rid of and thought they may come in handy for some of my students. I had a little play on Brian's kit while I was there which was fun.

As the years went on The Soul Detectives had various personnel changes. Mitch left after a short spell and Chris rejoined for a while followed by Dave Unwin. Chris also helped out for a while in 2004 when Dave had some time out. Finally Dave returned. We also had various brass players but Darren and Tony were our mainstay.

Chapter 13

Tony Jackson

In 2003 Tony Jackson's health was starting to concern me. He would call saying he did not think he had long to live. I would tell him not to be silly and that he would be fine. The truth was Tony knew he was very ill. He asked if I would take his guitars as he wanted me to have them. Again I told him he was overreacting and he would be fine.

Tony had a birthday coming up on 16th July. He was seven years older than me and would be 65. I made the decision to visit him in Nottingham as a surprise. I knew he never ventured out much any more so he would be in. Chris Halls said he would like to come with me so a cake and cards were purchased and off we went. The journey took several hours and finally we arrived at the address. Tony's flat was upstairs with his own stairway. I felt excited but also a little apprehensive as to what I would find. I went upstairs first and knocked on the door. The door was open but only about a foot. No reply. I knocked again and called out "Tony, it's Paul". He appeared from the small kitchen looking very surprised to see me and a little embarrassed at how he looked.

It was a shock. This was not the Tony I knew. The spell in prison had really taken its toll on his health. His face was sunken and he looked like an old man. We gave each other a hug. The door had been left open for the carer, a lady called Sue who Tony had asked to help him with shopping and cleaning. Tony had acquired more cats, about six in all. He really loved his cats; they were everywhere. I love animals but six cats in a flat!

We gave Tony the cake and cards and had a good long chat about the old times. Tony had trouble walking without the aid of a stick. His ankles had swollen up, but he still had his sense of humour. He told me a friend called Larry Williams also helped him. Tony had met him in a pub a few years before and if Tony needed to go somewhere Larry would drive him. It was handy for Tony plus Larry would be paid for his time.

Tony had various medications to take so it was good to have people who would collect them for him. After a few hours Chris and I said our goodbyes so that Tony could have a rest.

On our way home Chris said how shocked he was to see Tony in such a bad way. I was thinking exactly the same but I was so pleased we went for his birthday. Over the next few weeks it played on my mind. I had spoken to Tony on the phone and I had also spoken to Larry who confirmed that his condition had worsened. I needed to go back to visit again and on 17th August the day after Chris returned from holiday we went back to see Tony.

On our arrival Tony was in bed being attended to by a Macmillan nurse. In just four weeks his health had really deteriorated. He was pleased to see us and even wanted Chris to take a photo of him and me with his camera. Chris also took one on my camera. I have not included those photos in this book as he looked so ill and I would rather people remember him looking well. His cats sat on the bed with him and in various other chairs. They were good company for him. Poor Tony's arms were badly bruised from the medication and he was only drinking not eating solid food. His voice was very weak.

I made up my mind there and then that I would stay and sleep on the couch. Sue offered to put Chris up at her house. He could use one of her children's beds. I managed to make Tony laugh pulling faces and messing about as I did when we were on the road. Tony remarked that I would never change. I felt good having made him laugh.

Chris and I went to get something to eat at the fish shop. Larry stayed until we returned. We sat and had the fish and chips in the car so we were not out for very long. On our return the doctor called in to attend to Tony. Margaret and her son also called to see Tony. That day I managed to have a word with the doctor before he left. I asked how bad was it and the doctor said that Tony was very ill and could die within the next few days. His body was closing down. When he left I had to sit down and get my head around the bad news. Only Sue, Chris, me and Larry knew.

I helped Tony with his asthma inhalers. I also helped him go to the toilet. He was too weak to make it to the bathroom. There were small wet sponges to put in his mouth for moisture.

That evening Larry and I agreed that Tony's second wife, Christine, should be told. She and Tony had fallen out some time back. I managed to talk to Tony's ex father-in-law and he gave me Christine's number. We had a chat about Tony and it was good talking to her again. Christine was sad to hear of Tony's condition. It was arranged that the daughter and I would talk. I found her attitude amazing. OK they had fallen out but I explained her father was dying. Her attitude was "well what do you expect me to do". I took an instant dislike to her and for that reason will not even give her a name check. I know Tony was not the easiest of people at times but this was her chance to make amends with her dying father. I will never forgive her for that. This was the baby girl who had travelled with the band in our van when we were gigging in Europe all those years ago.

174

She was so aggressive in her voice. In the end I said I was only passing on the news and if she came now she would be able to talk to Tony before it was too late. "I cannot get time off work" was the reply, just like that. I put the phone down. I was so angry. Larry asked what she had said. He could not believe it when I told him. It really upset us.

Chris went to Sue's to stay that night and Larry went home. I helped Tony with his inhalers as he needed a couple of puffs. It was hard for Tony to talk. His voice was just a whisper. He was sitting up in bed making a gesture which I thought meant he wanted another puff on the inhaler. He was trying to tell me something but his voice was so weak. I could not understand what he was trying to say. He beckoned me to lean forward. As I did so Tony put his arms round me and hugged me. Here was a dying man saying thank you. It broke me up inside. It was the most wonderful experience. I felt so humble. Tony was being so brave.

The lady from the Macmillan nurses arrived. As the night went on we sat either side of the bed talking to Tony and holding his hands. The nurse said the hearing was always the last thing to go when a person is dying. She said Tony's breathing was very shallow and that there was not long to go. A couple of times we thought he had gone then he started breathing again. She said he was really fighting it. I told him to let go and be with his father who had not long died and to see his mother again. Telling him they were waiting for him. I did not want him to be frightened in his last moments. The nurse asked if I wanted to call Larry. I went to collect the number from my car. I ran and was only a couple of minutes.

The nurse was at the top of the stairs and said he died as you were going down stairs. It was about 45 minutes past midnight on 18th August 2003. I called Larry and the nurse called the doctor. I said I would like to have a few minutes alone with Tony. She asked if I was alright. I replied I was fine.

I thanked him for all the good times we had together and for being a good friend and that we all loved him. I went back into the lounge and it was not long before Larry arrived and the nurse made us a cup of tea. We were both gutted. It was hard to take in that Tony was no longer with us even though we had been expecting it. It was about forty minutes before the doctor arrived. He did not stay long. Poor Tony's body had just given up.

It was nearly two hours before the men from the Funeral Directors arrived. As we went into Tony's bedroom it was sad to see two of his cats lying on the bed with him. Tony was put into one of the body bags that I hate and find degrading. It reminded me of my father-in-law's death. It was not easy to manoeuvre Tony down the narrow stairs. He was put on a stretcher and at one point he was upright. It was difficult with the tight bend. Eventually Tony was carried out to the waiting car.

It was now early morning. Most people were still in bed. Once back in the flat we discussed what to do next. People would have to be told. We sat drinking lots of tea until it was OK to call people. I called Goldie, Mike Pender and Linda. Larry called Frank Allen of The Searchers and he said he would tell John McNally. Mike was saddened to hear the news. Everyone was. We had lost Ian, now Tony.

Frank Allen called back to speak to me about Tony. It was not long before the newspapers got hold of the story but unfortunately it was wrongly reported in many papers that Tony died in hospital. The coverage that Tony received was amazing. He must have been looking down with a big smile on his face. Probably saying Old Jake can still do it. Unfortunately a lot of the press were negative about his drinking problems forgetting the great records he made and his unique voice. Tony could sing Little Richard with the best of them. This prompted me to write and record a song called 'Jump Back'.

JACKSON: Chart-topper

Searchers star dies

SIXTIES pop star Tony Jackson of Merseybeat band The Searchers died yesterday, aged 64. He had cirrhosis of the liver and had suffered two heart attacks.

Three-times-married Jackson was vocalist and bass guitarist with the band during the early stages of its career.

He had his first chart-topping success in 1963 with Sweets For My Sweet. But to the surprise of fans he quit soon after the band's second No 1 hit, Needles And Pins, in 1964.

On the back of his success with The Searchers, he formed Tony Jackson And The Vibrations but did not hit the upper reaches of the charts again.

He lived with his five cats in a flat outside Nottingham.

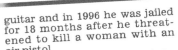

Searchers star Tony is dead

By Mark Reynolds

FORMER pop star Tony Jackson of The Searchers died yesterday aged 65.

The one-time vocalist and bass guitarist, who made a fortune with the group before suffering ill health, died shortly after midnight.

He had been taken to hospital near his home in Nottingham over the weekend with cirrhosis of the liver following years of hard drinking.

While The Searchers are one of the few groups to have survived the Sixties era and are still touring, Jackson – who quit the band in 1964 through illness – had fallen on hard times.

A series of health problems had left him unable to walk without the aid of a stick or even play his guitar and in 1996 he was jailed for 18 months after he threatened to kill a woman with an air pistol.

It emerged that Jackson telephoned the original members of the group last week to tell them

Tony Jackson: 'Wild man'

that he was dying. Band leader John McNally, 62, said: 'Because The Searchers had a very clean-cut image no one ever really knew that Tony was the wild man of the band in the Sixties.

'Growing up around The Beatles and with those times in Germany all of us liked a drink, but sadly Tony didn't know when to stop.

'He couldn't perform any longer because he was asthmatic but he was a good lad. He rang me last week to say he didn't have long left but he was still laughing and joking.'

The Searchers had 14 hits in the Sixties including three number ones – Sweets For My Sweet, Needles And Pins and Don't Throw Your Love Away.

Tony's flat was owned by the Council and Larry said we needed to start sorting things out. Chris and I stayed all day with Larry and Sue to help put things in some sort of order. There was so much to sort through. Larry found some old Christmas cards Tony's daughter had made and sent him when she was little. He had kept them all that time. That made me even angrier towards her.

We found an old calendar with big breasted ladies on it and that put a smile on our faces. It reminded me of the time while on tour in the 60's with Tony, me and a buxom lady!

By the end of the day we were all tired. We had been up all night and the energy level was low. Our main concern was Tony's cats. Most had gone out and not returned. A local cat rescue promised to find homes and if possible keep some together. Cages with food were put out and gradually most of them were found. A donation was made to the cat rescue on behalf of Tony. Chris and I finally made our journey back to Essex arriving in the evening quite exhausted by the whole experience.

Once back home Larry and I spoke regularly on the phone. He still had a lot of sorting out to do before the flat was handed back to the Council. There was also all the funeral arrangements to be made and the will with the Solicitors. Some of Tony's belongings were auctioned off for charity some months later.

People were very shocked to hear of his death. One fan, Jo Anne, came over from America especially for his funeral. On the day of the funeral Goldie, Chris, Marianna and I travelled up in one car. We drove to Larry and Ann's then went in one of the funeral cars to Wilford Hill Cemetery. We met Mike there.

It was a very big chapel. It had been arranged that Mike Pender, Larry, Chris and I would be pall-bearers. It was something we all wanted to do. Poor Larry nearly tripped at one point entering the chapel. It was a long way to carry the coffin to the stand at the front of the chapel. For some reason because of its size it reminded me of a cathedral. There were large iron gates and it had a high ceiling.

I was really pleased that John McNally and Frank Allen were there. Unfortunately they were not on speaking terms with Mike Pender. I found that very sad and thought this was the one time they could for Tony's sake. Tony loved Roy Orbison so a track by him was played along with 'Sweets for My Sweet' which brought a lump to my throat and I expect everybody else's as well. It was a lovely service to celebrate Tony's life. We had arranged for a guitar made of white flowers and it looked great.

Standing outside a TV camera crew were interviewing people. I gave them an interview and told them Tony had left a fantastic legacy of work and how much bands had been inspired by him and The Searchers. Mike paid Tony a nice tribute. Tony was cremated and I hope at peace with his Mum, Dad and brother. His ashes were eventually put with his family in Liverpool.

Left:
Mike Pender,
Linda Jackson,
Paul

Frank Allen wrote a nice tribute to Tony on The Searchers' website.

I have the guitars he wanted me to have and the lovely painting. But most of all the great memories of all the good times we had together. In his younger day Tony would take on the world but he mellowed as he got older and there was a lovely soft side to him and that is the way I want to remember him.

I am so grateful that I was able to be there for him at the end. Unfortunately a few years later Larry also died.

It is nice to know that people still enjoy listening to the records that Tony and the band made. One night while playing with The Soul Detectives at a venue in Maldon two men in their twenties came to speak to me. They produced several singles of Tony's and asked if I would sign them. They said at the Mod rallies Tony's music was always being played which was very pleasing to hear.

Chapter 14

The Soul Detectives, Hugh Attwooll and Latter Years

The Soul Detectives played gigs mainly in the East Anglia area and we were doing less in pubs and more private functions. The band had started out doing all soul material and gradually we brought in different styles. The Latin numbers always went down well so tracks by Santana and Paul Simon were added to the set list. These were also great for Darren's percussion.

The English weather did not suit Debbie, Darren's wife. It caused many problems with her asthma and eventually they were advised to try a country with a different climate. Debbie had lived in Australia as a child and had an Australian passport so after a lot of thought and a couple of visits to make sure they decided to emigrate in 2004. Darren ran his own Driving School in England and would do the same in Australia.

We were all happy that Debbie would have a better quality of life but were gutted at Darren leaving the band. He was such an integral part of it. We had about eight months to find another singer. We started auditioning vocalists. That was terrible. Some of the people were not up to it. It is not just the vocal side it is also the ability to communicate with an audience, which was the one thing that Darren had in abundance. We had one chap from Wales who had a good voice but he was still not what we were looking for.

Darren was due to leave for Australia in October so the band decided to give him a Christmas party at my rehearsal studio on Friday 20th August. We decorated the studio and had a Christmas tree complete with lights and fairy. Guests were invited to buy presents for Darren and Debbie but to pay no more than £5 and to be something silly.

On our first trip to Gabon there was also a children's entertainer from Colchester, Keith known as Mr. Nutty. We invited him to the party and asked if he could do some magic or something. He suggested dressing up as Father Christmas which was great and completed the theme.

We had current band members and partners and also invited past members and deps that knew Darren; about 20 guests. We had several tables put together so we could all sit down for the full Christmas dinner complete with turkey and Christmas pudding. Chris Halls cooked the turkey for us. We even managed to get crackers.

It was a fantastic surprise for Darren and Debbie. Darren did not recognise Keith at first when he was handing out the presents to them. It was only when he took his beard off that Darren realised who it was. A couple of the other band members had not twigged either. It was a great evening and they would have had their English Christmas, albeit a little early!

Before Darren left we managed to get together and had photos taken in the garden; it was a sad occasion for all of us. We had had so many laughs during Darren's time in the band. Darren's driving school in Australia has done well and he has made regular appearances on TV discussing topics on driving and safety.

Darren and I had also done some song writing together. I had written a song called Trina for a friend of Goldie's who had terminal cancer. In 2002 I finished up completing a whole CD called Pablo. Trina was able to hear the song before she died. The Soul Detectives and various musicians were used. Nick Pynn from the Steve Harley days played violin and a friend of his played cello.

Darren and family left for Australia in October and Mal a vocalist who was from another soul band in the Southend area helped us out for a couple of months. I think the band would have folded if he had not helped out. He did a good job but always reminded us of Norman Wisdom for some reason.

Our first gig without Darren felt very strange not only vocally but we also missed his percussion. The communication with the audience was terrible. Fred and Tina did their best but it fell way short of what we should be.

We were starting to tread water and needed a good front man again. Maria, one of the girl singers said she knew someone who may be what we were looking for. He had been at a gig and when the singer in the band held the mic to the audience his voice had come over well. So Richard came along for an audition. He had never sung with a band before, just some Karaoke in bars.

It turned out that he was already a fan of The Soul Detectives and used to come and watch us playing in Southend at the Riga Music Bar. Richie sounded good and the audition went well. It was such a relief after months of looking. He was right under our noses.

The band began to pick up again but it was not long before Fred left and was replaced by John Field. Then Tina left and we were back to a seven piece. Things gradually got back to normal with The Soul Detectives. Loosing Darren and Fred had been hard but John had settled in on guitar. Fred also had a great voice and we missed that but we soldiered on learning new material. Over the years the band had recorded several CDs. We always found the live ones to be our best.

Early in 2007 my good friend Hugh Attwooll who had been the drummer in The End before I joined, was diagnosed with cancer. We were all worried about him and I called him regularly. In June Goldie and I were due to go on holiday to Stockholm and Oslo and had only booked for 6 days instead of a week. Hugh did not sound too good the day before we left and I phoned Dave Brown in Cornwall, the bass player in The End/ Tucky Buzzard, and we both agreed we should visit Hugh on my return.

When we arrived back home on the Sunday there was a message to call Dave. Dave said Hugh was back in hospital and that we should go the next day, Monday 11th June. I cancelled my lessons for that day and we arranged to meet at Reading station. The next morning I went to buy my rail ticket and was informed of a problem on the line. Someone had jumped in front of a train. I was asked if I really needed to travel to which I replied that I did and I would wait for the line to clear.

Dave had a similar conversation at his station in Cornwall due to delays on the line to London and he also said that he needed to travel that day. The strange thing is with delays on both lines we still arrived at pretty much the same time. Colin a former member of The End met us at the station and took us to the hospital in Reading.

Hugh did not know that we were coming and he was very pleased to see us but was concerned that we had come such a long way. Bless him. It was terrible to see him so ill. We had to leave after twenty minutes to let a nurse attend to him. We managed to have a few minutes with him later on but Hugh was quite tired by then and needed more attention. One of the nurses was Spanish and had seen Hugh and the band play in Spain. What a small world. She was very sweet and we asked her to take special care of our friend.

Above:
Nicky, Jim,
Paul, Terry,
Hugh, Dave

Hugh died later that night. If Dave and I had not come that day we would not have seen him. Also if I had been away for 7 days it would have been too late. Everyone was gutted. Hugh was such a special person. Hugh and I had played a whole show together with Tucky Buzzard in JJ's Club in Madrid. It was great fun having two drummers do the whole night. We did a solo together for the finale which we both really enjoyed.

Hugh's ex-wife Melissa called to discuss the funeral arrangements. Hugh was to be cremated. We talked about what music to use. Melissa asked me to choose something which I thought he liked. Hugh and I both loved Buddy Rich so a track by his big band was one piece.

Hugh and I once went to see Buddy Rich with his big band at Ronnie Scott's Jazz Club in London. As usual he was fantastic and the band sounded so good. He would always have young gifted players with him. From where we were sitting we could see the dressing room door with a No Entry sign. Hugh said he would love to meet Buddy. My old tutor Frank King had died and Buddy, Kenny Clare and Louis Bellson had played a benefit concert for his family. I told Hugh that it would be a good idea to thank Buddy for doing that. Frank had been a chain smoker and walking into the small drum room in the cellar of Footes Shop in London took your breath away.

So we plucked up the courage to go in. Buddy was really nice. I told him I had been a student of Frank's and that seemed to help. Buddy was in a dressing gown about to have a meal. He was in a good mood and we walked out of there on cloud nine. I have spoken to well-known drummers who had also been very nervous of meeting Buddy. He had a reputation of being hard on people sometimes, but it was usually down to them not pulling their weight. Buddy was a perfectionist with a God given talent to play the drums, which he did from about 18 months old. He was back on the bandstand within months of having a triple bypass heart operation. An amazing man. Again I am so pleased Hugh had the chance to meet him. Over the years I was fortunate enough to meet Buddy several times to get programmes signed. It was always a huge pleasure to watch him play.

I also selected some music from The Mission soundtrack which finished with a drum like a heart beat. This would be the final piece before the coffin went behind the curtain. Tracks that Hugh had played on were played as mourners entered the chapel. Melissa asked if I would play a snare drum piece when the coffin was brought in. It was the hardest thing I have done in my music career. When I saw the coffin carried in with a snare drum on top my hands were shaking with emotion. Former band member Gordie Smith had made the coffin for Hugh. He did Hugh proud.

It was decided that the curtains would be left open as the people filed out of the church. I was able to place my drum sticks on top of the coffin. I asked one of the funeral directors to place the sticks inside the coffin.

Hugh was so loved by everyone. He had worked for CBS Records and was responsible for bringing Julio Iglesias to England. Hugh was very well respected in the industry.

The one thing he always loved was his drums. It was nice to see old friends at the funeral. Len and Charlie had travelled from Spain to be there.

After the service we went back to Hugh's daughter Helen's house where there was a marquee set up by the river. Her sister Claire and mother Marian, Hugh's first wife, were also at the funeral. In the early 70's Goldie and I were witnesses at their marriage in London and we gave them a wedding breakfast at our flat. It only seemed like yesterday.

Nicky got up and said nice things about Hugh which was very brave of him. It must have been hard. The strange thing is I thought I saw a bird fly in the open door of the marquee. In fact I did see it but as I looked again there was no sign of it. There was a full size cardboard cut out of Hugh along with many photos. It was as if he was still with us. Gordie and his sons had made the cut out and he brought it to my 60th birthday party in the October and we all paid our respects to Hugh again. It would have been Hugh's 60th in August.

On arriving back home I sat in the kitchen and saw a huge butterfly for a split second then it was gone. That night I had a really vivid dream. It was a lovely sunny day. Hugh was dressed in a smart suit standing talking to me and throwing a stick for his dog. He said what a lovely day it was. Melissa told me months later that while she was sorting out Hugh's belongings a large bird was sitting on a branch outside the window. It was one she had not seen before. After arriving home in America she saw the bird again in her garden.

Melissa asked if there was anything I would like of Hugh's. I replied I would like just one drum stick. That stick now resides in my studio. It is nice to have a reminder there of Hugh every time I sit at my kit. Students often ask me why I have a single stick up there and I tell them that it belonged to a very dear friend.

In 2005 and again in 2009 I was asked by the Trinity Guildhall School of Music to write some examination pieces for drum kit for their new grade books which came out in 2007 and 2011. I enjoyed doing that. The books go to over fifty countries around the world. It is great to think that someone in India may be doing one of my pieces for their exam.

I had already written two books for Orchard Percussion Studio students; Syllabus One in 2002 and Syllabus Two in 2004. I also produced a book and CD in 2004 called Drum Time Play Along for students to read and play along to parts.

Jack Bruce's son started drum lessons with me and had them for nearly three years. I also got the chance to gig with Jack again at a party in a marquee at his house. All his children are very talented musicians and vocalists.

Left:
Paul and Jack.
Paul's 60th
party 2007

The drum school had built up over the years and other tutors were required to clear the back log of people waiting for lessons which I could not fit in. We also had many well-known world class drummers doing master classes and clinics for us including Dave Weckl, Peter Erskine, Stanton Moore, Steve Smith, Jojo Mayer and Thomas Lang. It was and still is great for the students to be able to see up close what these drummers are doing. I also got to jam with Steve and Stanton which was fun.

Left:
Clem, Steve,
Paul

In 1999 we held our first 60 hour non-stop Drumathon to raise money for charity. There were about 150 drummers who were sponsored to play non-stop for an hour. All three studios were used over the weekend and we raised over £14,000 for Music for Unicef. The money went to help children in war-torn Bosnia. We held an evening of celebration at The Twist in Colchester when we handed over the cheque. The Soul Detectives entertained and Steve Harley came along to do some numbers with us.

The next two in 2002 and 2005 raised about £21,000 each for East Anglia's Children's Hospices. We had support from the local press, television and radio stations. I was very proud of everyone raising so much money. We even had drummers coming straight from their gigs to help me do the "graveyard shift" through the night. There is a fantastic camaraderie amongst drummers which I think is not found with other musicians.

Above:
Bill, Paul,
Goldie

Over the years Goldie and I attended a couple of parties at Bill Wyman's Sticky Fingers Restaurant in London. They were always great fun and full of so many well-known faces. We also attended Bill's surprise 60th Birthday Party on 22nd October 1996 which was superbly arranged by his wife Suzanne at the 100 Club in Oxford Street. Bill had no idea and the Club was full of family and friends. Jimmy Tarbuck was particularly funny in his speech and Peter Frampton got up and played a couple of songs with the band. For his 70th in October 2006 Bill had hired Ronnie Scotts Jazz Club and we were again invited.

Goldie and I had arranged for a ginger cake to be made and decorated and I was going to take it up to Bill at Gedding. This was all arranged with Mike who works for Bill so Bill had no idea I was going. I asked Jack Bruce if he fancied coming with me as a special surprise to which he agreed.

We drove up in Jack's Bentley. Jack stood behind me as we walked in so Bill did not see him at first. It was a great surprise for him and finally I had got one back on Bill for the surprise he pulled on me in the restaurant in America all those years ago.

Bill invited Jack to his 70th party at Ronnies. Ronnies had just been refurbished and looked great. Bill's band played with several people guesting including Jack. A lot of guests had come from abroad for the party including Roger Moore plus Donald 'Duck' Dunn the bass player who had influenced so many people including Bill. It was a fabulous evening and we spent a long time chatting and dancing with Cleo Rocos, who was lovely. She appeared in many of the Kenny Everett shows. We stayed in the Shaftesbury Hotel that night which was great not having to travel home.

The Soul Detectives did a fantastic reunion on 21st April 2007 when Darren visited the UK. We played at the Canvey Conservative Club where the band had a big following. The first set was with the original line up including Chris Teeder on keyboards, Fred on guitar and Tina joining Darren on vocals. We never rehearsed for Darren's set and it sounded great even after three years. Just as if he had never been away. The second set was with the current members. It was a great evening.

On 10th January 2009 Mick's wife, Evelyn, died. Handbags and Gladrags was her favourite song so various members of The Soul Detectives along with Fred on vocals recorded it for Ev's funeral. I was very pleased with the finished track. Fred did a first class job on vocals.

The Soul Detectives took their final bow on 3rd April 2010 with me as drummer after 17 years since I first formed the band. It had become completely dysfunctional and nobody could agree on anything. I felt that the band had run its course and the time had come to move on. Mick the bass player left at the same time.

Fred, Mick, Chris, Darren and I still work as the Original Soul Detectives whenever Darren is in the U.K. We had another reunion in 2011 with gigs at Canvey Conservative Club and Riga Music Bar.

Over the years I have had the honour of meeting some great musicians. In 2010 I had the chance to meet Steve Gadd who is admired by drummers all over the world, and to see him in clinic a few hours later. Yard, who does drum technician work with Steve and other drummers whilst on the road, has become a good friend of ours and is someone I would trust completely. There are not many people you can say that about. It is no surprise that he works with and is respected by so many big artists.

I love Steve's playing and he is a very humble person which is a bonus. There is a genuine love for him throughout the music business and huge respect for what he has achieved during his career. It is no surprise that Eric Clapton, Paul Simon and James Taylor all want him when they tour. He is a real inspiration to all musicians. You will never hear him overplay on a song; it's about leaving space so the music can breathe.

In 2010 Goldie and I celebrated 40 years of marriage. There are not many of our friends who are still with their first partners so we must be doing something right. Goldie reckoned she should have a third off for good behaviour and I said I should get a medal!

In May 2011 I took Marianna and Roy from Fuzzy Duck to Portugal to take her brother Ian's ashes to a place of rest. Roy was a close friend of Ian's. Being half Portuguese Ian always wanted to retire to Portugal, so it was fitting that his ashes go there. It had been a long time since he died in 1987. We all miss him. I expect he is up there jamming with Tony now. Ian made beautiful guitars. He would spend ages getting them just right.

It is on the cards that Roy, Mick and I will write some more 'Duck' numbers and release a second Fuzzy Duck CD.

As I approach my 64th birthday in October it is hard to think I have been playing drums for over fifty years. I still love it as much today as when I first started. 2009, was a special year for me as three of my students did very well. Cameron Morrell won best drummer in a competition at the Colchester Institute. Glen Little, a Lance Corporal in the Scots Guards took over as Principle Percussionist of the band. He is the youngest person to hold the position. Finally, Richard Rayner won the Young Drummer of the Year title.

I am so proud of them. They have all worked hard and deserve their success. What you have to have is a passion. It must start from there and then years of learning your craft. I have no time for students without that passion and who do not practice. They are time wasters.

I still love to try out new ideas. You never stop learning. One of my students is in his eighties and he is the same. Many former students have gone into teaching and are doing a good job, Emily, Mark, Matt, Richard, Stuart, Geoff, Adrian, Ben, Jim, Tom and many more. It pleases me that all that information is being passed on to future generations.

My former teachers, Ernie O'Malley, Frank King, and Jon Hiseman all helped me immensely. I will leave out the one who would leave tape recorders on in various rooms of the house for his students while he was outside cleaning his car! After a couple of lessons I went to the window and there he was! That was my last lesson with him. His passion was right out of the window!

I cannot thank my parents enough for letting me do what I wanted in life – to play the drums.   I have been extremely fortunate to have travelled the World meeting people doing something I love and being paid for it has been a bonus.   I have never taken that for granted.   Who would have thought from my first gig at a wedding in Kent all those years ago that one day I would get a chance to play Las Vegas, Madison Square Gardens, Carnegie Hall and Wembley Arena.   And work with so many great artists. What an amazing journey it has been.   I still love teaching and playing.   It is the one thing I do not get impatient with.   Big thanks go to Goldie for being there and never complaining.

Incidentally an amazing thing happened whilst writing this book. Completely out of the blue one day I received a phone call from Irving Martin. I had not had any contact with him since the Tony Jackson days; nearly 45 years ago! We had a good long chat and Irving said that he still gets regular enquiries from people about Tony and the recordings. It was lovely to know that there is still interest in Tony but it was very freaky that he should happen to ring me at that time after all those years.

I have also been very lucky to have companies like Zildjian, Sonor, Pro Mark and Protection Racket give me endorsements for their excellent equipment.

And so to all you budding drummers out there or anyone with a dream I say "Go for it. Live your dream. You are only here once. This is not a dress rehearsal. I sincerely hope you achieve your dream and I hope you enjoyed reading about mine."

PABLO

Paul Francis Discography

Singles

Tony Jackson and The Vibrations	Bye Bye Baby	Pye Records 1964
Tony Jackson and The Vibrations	You Beat Me to The Punch	Pye Records 1964
Tony Jackson and The Vibrations	Love Potion No. 9	Pye Records 1965
Tony Jackson and The Vibrations	Stage Door	Pye Records 1965
Bobby Rio and The Revelles	Don't Break My Heart and Run Away	Pye Records 1965
Tony JacksonGroup	You're My Number One	CBS Records 1966
Tony Jackson	Never Leave Your Baby's Side	CBS Records 1966
Tony Jackson Group	Follow Me	CBS Records 1966
Tony Jackson	Anything Else You Want	CBS Records 1966
The Compromise	You Will Think of Me	CBS Records 1966
Dave Walton	Every Window In The City	CBS Records 1966
Johnny Devlin	Prove It	CBS Records 1966
Screaming Lord Sutch	The Cheat	CBS Records 1966
Eddie's Crowd	Baby Don't Look Down	CBS Records 1966
Pepper	We'll Make It Together	Pye Records 1968
Miguel Rios	Rock de la Carcel	Hispavox Records 1970
Miguel Rios	You're All Alone (B side)	Hispavox Records 1970
Polo Opuestos	En el Verano	Hispavox Records 1970
Tucky Buzzard	You're All Alone	Hispavox Records 1971

Fuzzy Duck	Double Time Woman	MAM Records 1971
Fuzzy Duck	Big Brass Band	MAM Records 1971
Gilbert O'Sullivan	Underneath The Blanket Go	MAM Records 1971
Tranquility	Couldn't Possibly Be	Epic Records 1972
Redgie Seebo	Please Don't Bring Your Sister Tonight	Cube Records 1974
Geno Washington	End of The World	DJM Records 1975

E.Ps

Various Artists	The Hit Makers 1964	Pye Records 1965
Tony Jackson Group	Tony Jackson Group	Estudio Records 1967
Jackson Queen	Jackson Queen	Jackson Queen 1988

L.Ps

Miguel Rios	Despierta	Hispavox Records 1970
Miguel Rios	A Song of Joy	Hispavox Records 1970
Tucky Buzzard	Coming On Again	Hispavox Records 1972
Tucky Buzzard	Tucky Buzzard	Capitol Records 1971
Gilbert O'Sullivan	Spotlight On	MAM Records
Fuzzy Duck	Fuzzy Duck	MAM Records 1971

Chris Spedding	The Only Lick I Know	EMI Records 1972
Tranquility	Silver	Epic Records 1972
Brian Friel	Arrivederci Ardrossan	Dawn Records 1974
Mick Ronson	Play Don't Worry	RCA Records 1974
Maggie Bell	Suicide Sal	Polydor Records 1975
Tony Jackson Group	Just Like Me	Strange Things 1991
The End	The Last Word	Tenth Planet 2000

CDs

Steve Harley	Yes You Can	Food For Thought 1992
Steve Harley	Poetic Justice	CD Transatlantic 1996
Tucky Buzzard	Time Will Be Your Doctor	Castle Records 2005
Tucky Buzzard	Coming On Again	Ripple Records
Tucky Buzzard	Tucky Buzzard	Ripple Records
Maggie Bell	Live At The Rainbow 1974	Angel Air Records
Maggie Bell	Live In Boston, USA 1975	Angel Air Records
The Soul Detectives	Tracked	Soul Detectives 1996
The Soul Detectives	Carry On RIGArdless	Soul Detectives 2002
The Soul Detectives	Late In The Evening	Soul Detectives
Paul Francis	Pablo	Orchard Percussion 2002

Compilations

There are numerous compilation CDs out featuring various artists and tracks already listed.